A History of the Application of Islamic Law in Nigeria

Yushau Sodiq

A History of the Application of Islamic Law in Nigeria

palgrave
macmillan

Yushau Sodiq
Texas Christian University
Fort Worth, Texas, USA

ISBN 978-3-319-50599-2 ISBN 978-3-319-50600-5 (eBook)
DOI 10.1007/978-3-319-50600-5

Library of Congress Control Number: 2016962462

Printed on acid-free paper

This Palgrave Macmillan imprint is published by Springer Nature
The registered company is Springer International Publishing AG
The registered company address is: Gewerbestrasse 11, 6330 Cham, Switzerland

This work is dedicated to my beloved parents
Alhaji Sadiku Alagbede Onakoya
and
Alhaja Sinotu Iya Tule Sadiku,
and my beloved teacher,
Prof. Isma'il Raji al-Faruqi

Preface

Since my childhood I have developed a keen interest in law. I lived near a courthouse when I was young and always admired the way the lawyers and judges dressed and talked. I loved their professionalism. Later, when I attended university, I decided to specialize in law, and since I carried out my studies in Saudi Arabia I chose to study Islamic law, which is considered to be the pinnacle of all knowledge in Islam. I earned my BA, MA, and PhD degrees in Islamic law. Unfortunately, my father was unaware of my studies. He thought I was studying the *Qur'an* and *Hadith*, the subjects most commonly studied by Muslims. When he became aware of my specialization, he voiced his objection to it and discouraged me from practicing law and becoming a judge because of the negative attitude that people had about the lawyers in our community. Unfortunately, lawyers were perceived as agents of colonial rule because of their harsh treatment of their fellow citizens. As a result of my father's objection, I turned to teaching Islamic law at the University of Sokoto in Nigeria.

As I began teaching I found that many Nigerians, particularly southerners (I am a southerner myself), had no clue of what Islamic law is; they thought it was a branch of native law, which is undocumented. They began asking many uncritical questions about the nature of Islamic law and its relevance in Nigeria. This sparked my interest in writing about the history of Islamic law, its application and its critique, especially by non-Muslims. I also found that many people within and outside Nigeria have little knowledge, hold distorted views or make fallacious assumptions about Islamic law.

In undertaking this work I strongly believe that many people could benefit from it and that most of their misconceptions about Islamic law could be corrected or at least re-examined. Islamic law has its own uniqueness and dynamism, which cannot be compared to any other manmade law. It permeates all aspects of Muslim daily life and guides Muslims regarding what to do and what not to do. Nevertheless, it has a negative side and staunch critics who struggle to admire anything about it. These critics project Islamic law as an old and harsh legal system, which should be put aside and replaced by Western common law, which the majority of Muslims today believe has failed them. It is pertinent to mention here that Islamic law was in operation in Nigeria from the eighteenth century and it is the only written legal system, which the British colonial rulers found in operation in Northern Nigeria when they arrived. The British rulers retained and modified it, and thus it continues to operate today.

This book deals with the history of the application of Islamic law in Nigeria. It analyzes how Islamic law emerged in Nigeria toward the beginning of the nineteenth century and remained applicable until the arrival of the British Colonial regime in Northern Nigeria in 1903. It sheds light on how colonial rule retained Islamic law in Northern Nigeria, which led to its survival until today.

This research is unique in that it offers a brief history of the development of Islamic law in Nigeria, particularly in Northern Nigeria, where twelve states are using it; and how it was received and applied to all aspects of life from the nineteenth century until 1960 when Nigeria became an independent nation, and from 1999 until the present. It also details the composition of Islamic courts from native courts to area courts, and from *Shari`ah* courts to Shari`ah courts of appeal, which shows the progress that Islamic law has achieved in the last two centuries.

The great need for this book lies in the absence of concise scholarship and accessible literature on Islamic law in Nigeria. Also, most works on the subject are written purely by scholars who have had little familiarity with Islam and its laws. Because I am an insider, I have taught Islamic law in Northern Nigeria and I maintain contact with Islamic courts through former students who are now judges at various *Shari`ah* courts in the region, I am familiar with how Islamic courts apply Muslim laws. As a professor of Islamic legal and religious traditions at Texas Christian University, and as a scholar trained in both classical Islamic laws and Western education, I am uniquely equipped to enlighten both Muslims and non-Muslims regarding

Islamic law. Non-Muslims in the West have many misunderstandings about the *Shari`ah.*

This book is written primarily for those seeking basic knowledge about Islamic law, how and why it is applied in Nigeria, and the impact of such an application on Muslim and non-Muslim Nigerians. In particular, the arguments of both proponents and opponents of Islamic law are detailed in Chapters 2 and 3 to enable readers to evaluate the merits of each point of view and hence make their own decision regarding whether or not Islamic law benefits Nigerians. In sum, the book will enable readers to become knowledgeable about Islamic law in Nigeria. Readers will be given the resources to clearly recognize what Islamic law represents and to discern how it serves the needs of Nigerian citizens.

This book consists of six chapters.

Chapter 1 provides a short introduction to the history of Nigeria and its culture. It also defines what Islamic law is, why it has different shades of meaning and how it has developed from its beginning in the 1800s to today.

Chapter 2 addresses the history of Islam, how Islamic law was introduced into Nigeria and how Sokoto Caliphate (1808–1903) became the champion of the establishment of Islamic law across Northern Nigeria in the nineteenth and early twentieth centuries.

Chapter 3 examines the structure of Islamic law during British colonial rule and the impact that the British had on its application in Nigeria.

Chapter 4 describes examples of how Islamic law is practiced in the *Shari`ah* courts in Northern Nigeria. Four cases are studied.

Chapter 5 examines how Nigerian Christians respond to the application of Islamic law in Nigeria. It examines the objections raised by Nigerian Christians, particularly by those who are most fervent in condemning Islamic law, the Christian Association of Nigeria. Christians' objections are analyzed and Muslim responses are elaborated.

Chapter 6 evaluates how Islamic law is specifically practiced in Zamfara State with a critical analysis of its successes and failures.

The conclusion summarizes the main themes of the book and provides concluding thoughts.

The appendix provides the sections of 1999 Constitution of Nigeria that relate to Islamic law.

Hence the major contributions of this book are:

- It is the first short in-depth history of the application of Islamic law in Nigeria.
- It offers an analysis of the complexity and resilience of Islamic court systems in Northern Nigeria
- It contains numerous illustrations of how and why Islamic law has been applied in different areas of life
- It provides substantiating documentation of Islamic law procedures in *Shari`ah* Courts based on descriptions of actual court cases. It thus exposes the fallacious assumption that *Shari`ah* courts do not have written records.
- It demonstrates the popular evolution of Islamic law in Nigeria based on examples of how the application of Islamic law went through public debates before it was adopted and incorporated into the 1999 Constitution. Specifically, it argues not only that Islamic law was present in Nigeria and applied before British common law was introduced but also that Islamic law was not imposed on Nigerian citizens, as is alleged by the Western media.
- It offers a specific, user-friendly introduction to Islamic law, which can be accessed by specialists and non-specialists alike.

Acknowledgments

This work would not have seen the light of publication without the support of God and encouragement from many concerned colleagues, friends and family members. Only a few of them are mentioned here but to all of them I express my thanks.

Special thank go to my wife, Haleemat, for her patience with me during my academic career and particularly when I was working on this research on Islamic law. She has offered relentless assistance. I express my gratitude to my colleagues in the Department of Religion at Texas Christian University for their academic advice and continued encouragement. Special thanks go to Prof. Nadia Lahutsky for her enthusiasm and departmental financial support, Prof. Mark Dennis, Prof. Iysa Ade Bello, Prof. Akin Akinade for their support and encouragement, and to Prof. Jack Hill for reading my proposal and making constructive suggestions. I also thank Dr Scott Langston for proofreading the whole manuscript. As a result of his careful reading and valuable suggestions, this work received a warm reception from my publishing editors—Alexis Nelson and Amy Invernizzi. To both I express my thanks.

I also thank my colleagues at the Nigerian universities. They assisted me in collecting cases from the *Shari`ah* courts in Sokoto, Kano and Kwara states. Special appreciation goes to Prof. Sulayman Olawiyola Rabiu of Uthman Dan Fodio University, Prof. Zubair Abdul Qadir of University of Ilorin, Dr. Isa Ahmad of the Kwara State College of Legal Studies and to my friend, Mr. Muhsin Shaheed for his continued support.

There are several others who have assisted me in one way or another during my research. I thank them all.

Dr Yushau Sodiq

Contents

CHAPTER 1

Nigeria: The Giant of Africa

Introduction

Nigeria, the largest country in West Africa, is a land of diverse cultures and a nation of many peoples (e.g. the Fulani-Hausa, the Yoruba and the Igbos) with rich religious traditions. The name "Nigeria" was given to the country by Lord Luggard's wife in 1914.[1] Nigeria is bordered in the north by Niger Republic, in the south by the Gulf of Guinea, in the west by Benin and in the east by Cameron and Chad. Its present population is about 160 million and it has an area of 356,669 square miles. Its climate varies from region to region and generally there are two seasons: dry and wet, with different temperatures.[2] Nigerians speak a range of languages, including English (the official language), Hausa, Igbo and Yoruba. Within each of these major languages are many dialects. Only Hausa, Yoruba and Ibo are written languages. While both Ibo and Yoruba use Latin script, introduced by the British, Hausa was originally written in Arabic script, known as *ajami,* prior to the arrival of the British. Nigerian currency is called Naira and the government had dropped the use of coins. Major holidays in Nigeria are New Year's Day, Good Friday and Easter, *Eid al-Fitr* and *Eid al-Kabir* (Muslim festivals), Independence Day and Christmas Day. Unfortunately there is no "national day" for the indigenous religions, which have become overshadowed by Islam and Christianity, which rival one another in trying to win over the indigenes.

Y. Sodiq, *A History of the Application of Islamic Law in Nigeria*,
DOI 10.1007/978-3-319-50600-5_1

Nigeria is a federal republic. It won its independence from the British in 1960 and became a republic in 1963. At present it has 36 states and a federal capital at Abuja. Preceding its amalgamation in 1914 by the British, Nigeria has a long and rich history that goes back more than 3000 years. It boasted major empires in Africa with very rich traditions and cultures. Among its past empires were Oyo, Igbo, Kanem-Bornu and Hausa-Fulani. Each empire had its distinctive administrative structure and system of governance. In 1914 they all merged to form a cohesive government, Nigeria. The integration has not been successful because of the country's division into many states following independence. A citizen of one state cannot become a governor or senator in another state, hence the sense of unity or patriotism among Nigerians is always being challenged.

Although Nigeria claims to be a secular state, religious issues permeate all aspects of the population's private and public lives daily lives. Many religions are practiced in the country, and they shape both local and federal policies to a large extent. Nigeria has three major religions: Islam, which is predominant in the North, Christianity, which is predominant in the East and many parts of the West, and African indigenous religions, which have minority followers in many parts of Nigeria. Muslims account for about 48% of the population, Christians 40% and African traditional religions and others (e.g. Hinduism and Judaism) 12%.[3] Both Christianity and Islam are perceived as intolerant religions because of their contempt for indigenous religions, which they arrogantly label as paganism. On the other hand, Islam and traditional African religions are perceived as indigenous, as stated in the adage saying, *Aiye laba Ifa, aiye laba Imale, osan gangan ni Igbagbo wole de.* This means [we found both Ifa and Imale (Islam) in Nigeria as natural religions; Christianity just came in the afternoon.] Christianity and Islam are exclusive religions; they rival one another and occasionally resort to violence to achieve their missionary goals. The adherents to indigenous religions are the smallest group yet they influence Islam and Christianity because people resort to these beliefs during times of crisis. One of the causes of tension between Muslims and Christians is the introduction and application of the *Shari`ah* (Islamic law) in twelve northern states in 2000–2002. One of the major reasons why northerners resorted to the *Shari`ah* was the claim that Westernization and the use of "common law" did not bring peace to the country. Rather, they turned Nigeria into an immoral community with widespread corruption in the name of democracy. The issue of the application of Islamic law is yet to be resolved. There are other important causes of unrest in Nigeria, such as tribal and ethnic crises, corruption, unemployment and the terrorism of the Boko Haram group in the North-Eastern states of Nigeria. This group has threatened the stability of the Nigerian government. The new elected leader, President Muhammad Buhari, has vowed to rid Nigeria of Boko Haram and has thus aligned himself with neighboring countries, such as Chad, Niger and Cameron, to form a unified front against the terrorist group so that it will have no safe haven in the region.

Politically, Nigeria is a *recovering* democratic country.[4] It witnessed nineteen years of brutal military dictatorship and ten years of corrupt civilian rules. Following its independence in 1960, it has gone through many changes of government, from a British parliamentary system to an American presidential democratic system, from civilian to military dictatorial rule until May 29, 1999, when the people chose an elected leader, President Olusegun Obasanjo. Under his leadership, Nigeria became relatively stable and peaceful, although the country still occasionally experiences religious turbulence, ethnic crises, civil demonstrations and cult disturbances in colleges all over the country. The government tries to solve these issues amicably but its failure to tackle the roots of the problems hampers its efforts. The main causes are religious intolerance among Muslims and Christians, high rates of unemployment, mismanagement of resources and corruption of the elected leaders. President Muhammad Buhari, who took over on May 29, 2015, has promised to make a lot of changes to bring peace to Nigeria and to provide jobs for millions of the country's graduates, some of who turn to robbery and violence as a result of the lack of employment.

Nigeria continues to have good relationship with its neighbors. It maintains trade relationships with nearly all countries of the world and has embassies in those states. It is a member of many international organizations and it leads the world in international peacekeeping. Wherever one visits in the world, one finds Nigerians there. Unfortunately, the country has a bad image abroad owing to the corruption of a few Nigerians who engage in fraud and international drug trafficking. Nevertheless, Nigeria has produced great leaders who have contributed to the development of Nigeria. Among these are Sir Abu Bakr Tafawa Balewa, Dr. Nnamdi Azikwe, Michael Opara, Sir Ahmadu Bello, Chief Obafemi Awolowo, Major General Muritala Muhammad, General Muhammad Buhaari, Lateef Jakande and President Olusegun Obasanjo. The leader of the country today is the retired General Muhammad Buhari, who won the election in May 29, 2015. He succeeded Mr. Goodluck Jonathan, whose regime has been described as Nigeria's most corrupt government.

Economically, Nigerians are very hard-working people and they believe strongly in capitalism. The country is extremely rich in natural and human resources but suffers from corruption and mismanagement. Nigeria is the sixth largest crude oil producer in the world and 90% of its budget comes from oil revenue. Before the oil boom of 1973, Nigeria relied exclusively on agriculture, but later the government ignored it and relied heavily on the exportation of oil. A lack of adequate technological development has placed Nigeria into the group of underdeveloped countries, despite its abundant resources. Past civilian and military governments did not invest in the infrastructure of the country during the oil boom. Instead, the public sector was ignored and major requirements, such as electricity, good roads and communications, were not developed.

The government of President Obasanjo strove hard to develop Nigeria's economy by combating corruption and mismanagement in the government sectors. His efforts yielded some results. He also embarked on various serious development projects involving the country's infrastructure, and he invited Nigerians abroad and foreign investors to invest in Nigeria. During his presidency, he improved communication systems and privatized many government companies to boost their productivity and efficiency.

Nigerian people are naturally entrepreneurial, especially the Yorubas and Igbos. They engage in all types of business, and travel to any part of the world for trade. Women are the backbone of business in Nigeria and they control the local markets. However, they are under-represented in the public sector and in politics despite the fact that they represented more than 50% of the voters at the general elections of 2003 and 2015. President Buhari has promised to boost the economy, provide jobs and eliminate corruption as much as possible. Many Nigerians today have great hope for a bright future under his new government.

Nigerians take education seriously. The country has produced many scholars, educators and artists in all fields of science, technology, law, religion, history, engineering and so forth. There are Nigerian professors, doctors, artists, educators and lawyers all over the world. Even though there is still some illiteracy, the government continuously strives to provide free primary and secondary education for its citizens. Nigeria today has more than 120 universities, hundreds of technical schools, colleges of education and polytechnics, and thousands of elementary and high schools, with more than 20 million students in primary schools, 9 million students in secondary schools and about 1.8 million students in colleges in 2010. The adult literacy rate is about 61% for people aged fifteen years and older.

There are thousands of Nigerians in undergraduate and graduate colleges in the USA, the UK and Europe. Attention is now also being paid to science and technology.

Nigerians begin their informal education at home and formal education at the age of six. They spend six years in elementary (primary level), three years in junior high and three years in senior high (secondary level). Interested students pursue higher education at one of the government or private universities, which lasts for four years. Every graduate student from university enrolls in national youth community service for a year following graduation. Many Nigerians study abroad. After completion of their degrees, some return home while others remain abroad to work.[5]

Each ethnic group in Nigeria boasts its own culture and ways of life. Although some of these cultures are similar in some ways, each has its own unique features. For instance, the sculptures of the Nok people of Jos Plateau and Zaria are a source of admiration; and the bronze works of the Yoruba in Ile-Ife and Benin, especially the heads of the kings, are fascinating. Each group maintains unique ceremonies: Egungun, Gelede, Bori and other entertainments, such as mask, Sakara, Fuji, Apala dances and *boju-boju* (cover the eyes' games) are sources of pride and amusement for spectators. Nigerians make decorative carvings from wood, calabash (from Oyo), stone, ivory and bones. In addition, marriage, birth and funeral ceremonies in each community differ from one another. These art forms are found in many regions and reflect the ancient traditions of the country.[6] Furthermore, Nigerians produce theater plays and films such as *The Lion and the Jewel* by Wole Soyinka, who won the Nobel Prize for Literature in 1986. There are other Nigerians whose works have earned them respect and recognition all over the world, including Chinua Achebe, whose novel *Things Fall Apart* has been translated into many languages.

Nigeria has produced great scholars in all fields of education and the sciences. Nigerian Nollywood has won great admiration by the film industry all over the world for its quality and characters.[7]

The Meanings of Islamic Law (*Shari`ah*)

Human beings are social creatures. They are created to relate to one another. As they live together, they enjoy one another but occasionally step on each other's toes. They disagree on certain issues, which may be serious or trivial. Eventually, the strong wants to exercise his power over the weak, while the weak tries to escape the wrath of the strong. Hence, in a civil society, rules are laid down to regulate human relationships. Laws are enacted to set the boundaries of each and to define what is legitimate, lawful or prohibited. If people adhere to these rules, they live peacefully; if they ignore them, chaos sets in and disturbs the societal peace which human beings yearn for. These rules and regulations, which govern the relationships of each individual with his fellow human beings, are the laws. They are established according to the needs of the members of each society. Hence different societies follow different laws. The more complex a society becomes, the larger and more expansive its laws become. There is no society without laws, even in tribal communities. These laws are written or understood by the leaders of the different societies. Society as a whole requires each individual to abide by the law in order to keep peace. Nevertheless, every law changes as a result of the needs of the people, and the emergence of new things, developments or circumstances which warrant the change. The law thus endows humans with the freedom to live and relate to one another peacefully. The law should not be comprehended as a tool of restriction, as some may perceive it to be; rather, it is a means of guaranteeing to each individual their rights. At the same time, law distinguishes itself from moral ethics.

Law generally encompasses any rule that governs the relationship between members of a society, but it is backed up by punishment for its violation. When a driver drives in a civil society, he follows traffic rules. That is the law. He who violates traffic laws receives a ticket and pays a fine, if caught. The fine results from his failure to abide by the law set down to protect human lives. The fine differs from one state to another and from one country to another. Regardless, everyone pays for such violation. The above example represents the meaning of law in the West, a rule that is established and then backed up by a punishment. On the other hand, rules that are created to encourage people to be better citizens and compassionate human beings are known as "moral or ethical laws," because failure to comply with them incurs no punishment. Thus, for example, helping a beggar or homeless person on the street constitutes a moral issue. Failure to help them, even though one has the means to do so, would not subject someone to any punishment because there is no law forcing a citizen to assist the homeless. This is the responsibility of an established government. Individuals are free to choose whether or not to help.

Human beings cannot live peacefully together without establishing laws to govern their daily affairs. It is on this basis that Islam sets down rules to regulate the affairs of its adherents. Islam evokes strong criticism whenever its laws are discussed because they are perceived to be old and not adaptable to the modern world. Western scholars argue that Islamic law can hardly meet the needs of the modern age. Muslims for their part reject this as an inadequate understanding of Islam, arguing that Islamic law can be applied today and can meet the needs of its members because it is flexible enough to accommodate new rules and provide legal solutions to new problems that the Muslim world is facing. But what is Islamic law (*Shari`ah)* and how has it developed? Can it be applied today despite its condemnation by many?

Shari`ah* literally means [the road to the river.] The root word *shara'a* means to introduce, to enact and to prescribe a law. Whenever the term *Shari`ah is used, it connotes the law which God has promulgated through the Prophet Muhammad. It represents the totality of God's commandments relating to the activities of human beings, apart from those relating to ethics. In other words, Islamic law is:

> The canonical law of Islam as put forth in the *Koran* and the *Sunnah* and elaborated by the analytical principles of the four orthodox schools (*madhhab*, pl. *madhahib*), the Shafi'i, Hanafi, Hanbali, and Maliki, together with that of the Shi'ites, the Ja'fari.[8]

Muslims believe that Islamic law is the law of God, revealed in the *Qur'an* and explained by the Prophet Muhammad. It is guidance for humanity in all its affairs. Muslims are required to follow this law in order to live a peaceful and prosperous life. They believe that as water is the source of life, following the laws of God, the *Shari`ah*, is a means of living a peaceful and harmonious life. It can give Muslims a profound sense of security and stability.

Basically, Islamic law covers two essential aspects of human life: the secular and the religious, the sacred and the profane (*ibadat* and *mu'amalat*). The religious rules (*ibadaat*) deal with a human's duties towards God, like religious observances, such as belief, prayer, almsgiving, fasting and pilgrimage to Mecca. This area of religious law is not considered important in the West because it is perceived to be a private matter with which the law of the state does not interfere. However, in Islam, there is no separation between the state and the Church, so Islamic law covers all aspects of life and prescribes for believers what they should and should not do regarding their relationship with God and their spiritual life. Their failure to obey God in this religious area may subject them to punishment in this world or in the next, if they do not repent. These are religious laws and Muslims pay great attention to them.

The transactional laws (*mu'amalat*) are those pertaining to the material world, such as criminal law, contract law, family law, civil law and property law.[9] The general rules governing these are mentioned in the *Qur'an* and the *Sunnah*, the traditions of the Prophet Muhammad. Muslims are required to obey these rules as promulgated in the revealed message. They believe that since God creates humans, He knows what is best for them. It is out of love and mercy that God prescribes for them what they should do and what they should not do so as not to go astray:

> Then we put you on the right way of religion. So follow that way, and follow not the desires of those who know not. (*Qur'an* 45:18)

Of course, the execution and interpretation of the laws of God lie in the hands of the Muslim jurists (*ulama'*) and leaders. They are charged with promoting justice and fair dealing in a society. *The main purpose of Islamic law is the establishment of a just society, prevention of evil deeds and protection of all members of the society from danger, whether they are Muslims or not.*

Even though the Muslim scholars define the *Shari`ah* in different ways, they all come to the conclusion that it is the law that governs all aspects of a Muslim's life, both sacred and profane, and how they should live their lives in relation to other members of the society. It should be pointed out that the whole of the *Shari`ah* is not revealed law; some parts are revealed and others are inferred from the revealed ones. Regardless of whether the *Shari`ah* is revealed or not, its application needs human interpretation, which is very subjective. And since the basic laws which the primary sources (the *Qur'an* and the *Sunnah*) mention are limited, and the human problems are unlimited and unpredictable, the revealed laws have to be expanded to cover novel issues that are not addressed by the text. Therefore Islamic law is ever evolving and is thus subject to re-evaluation to serve the purposes which it is supposed to serve. The repeated claim that Islamic law has never changed has no validity because any scholar who is familiar with its history can easily recognize the many developments that Islamic law has gone through. A cautionary note can also be made here that even though Islamic law has gone through many changes and reinterpretations, one should not conclude that the whole package of Islamic law is a manmade product, as some have alleged. Rather, the Prophet Muhammad received the basic foundations of Islamic law from God; he added his own interpretations to them; and after his death his companions extended those laws to areas which Muhammad had not addressed. As a result, Islamic law was expanded. Denying the divine aspect of Islamic law is thus tantamount to denying the whole of Islam. What can safely be asserted is that some parts of Islamic law are revealed while others are inferred through human interpretation of the divine message. In such interpretation, human intellect is employed.

Since the *Shari`ah* consists of both revelation and human interpretation, should a Muslim follow *Shari`ah* law or not? There are different answers to this question. One is that the *Shari`ah* covers two major areas: religious laws (*ibadat*) and transactional laws (*mu'amalat*). Religious laws are the laws which cover the relationship between human beings and God, such as how to pray, how to fast and how to get close to God. In these areas, Muslim scholars opine that a Muslim has to learn how God wants to be related to. Since Muhammad said that God has to be worshipped five times daily, Muslims worship Him five times daily. It would not be acceptable to choose to worship only three times. Even though the rules which regulate humans' relationship with God would not be considered law in the Western concept, Muslims accept such rules as laws that must be obeyed. Any violation of them subjects a Muslim to a certain punishment. In these religious laws, Muslims have to obey them and comply with them to win the Mercy of God. To Muslims, God has some involvement in their daily lives.

The other aspect of law is that which regulates humans' relationship with one another. There are some basic principles given by God that must be followed, while there are other areas where humans are left to decide for themselves what is good. Where there are suggestive rules by God, Muslims are also free to adapt the law to their circumstances as long as they keep the spirit of the law (*maqasid al-Shari`ah*) in mind.

The Development and Emergence of the Islamic Law

Human beings are by their nature evolutionary creatures: they never stop developing. As they develop, their laws change too. Many people think that Islamic law has never changed since it was revealed to the Prophet Muhammad in the seventh century (CE). A critical study of the history of Islamic law shows that it has changed considerably at different times as a result of the expansion of Islam and various needs of the Muslim community. Change is a natural phenomenon of everything. The only thing that Muslims believe does not change is God Himself. Yet He revealed different laws to different nations according to their needs. Islamic law has gone through many developments since its advent, and it will continue to change to accommodate the ever-growing needs of human beings at different times. Muslim scholars have argued that Islamic law has gone through at least five major stages of development.

The Period of the Prophet Muhammad

When Muhammad began to receive his revelations from God in Mecca, he was instructed by God to explain the meaning of his message to his followers. Initially, the revelation at this stage, particularly in Mecca, emphasized the belief in the oneness of God, the reality of death, and resurrection on the Day of Judgment. He affirmed the importance of committing oneself to religion by doing good deeds and forbidding evil acts, and developing moral values, such as trust and fairness. These beliefs and rules are expressed in terms of admonition and warning with no punishment attached to them during the Meccan period. Muhammad encouraged his followers to apply whatever he taught them, and he emphasized personal moral development. At that time there was no Islamic state to implement any form of Islamic law; Muslims were in the minority in Mecca. Muslim scholars referred to this stage as the stage of laying the foundation. Muhammad spent thirteen years in Mecca inviting his people to Islam, before he immigrated to Medina in 622 CE to escape his persecution by the people of Mecca, the Quraysh, who had vowed to assassinate him.

The people of Medina received him warmly and he became the leader of the city as Muslims grew in number. Eventually he began to regulate the society. He continued to receive revelations but with a great shift in emphasis towards the social, economic and political spheres of the Muslim community. He introduced new laws regarding the religious aspects of Islam; he explained rules regarding family structure; he elaborated on social economic needs and how members had to support one another through almsgiving to the poor (*Zakat*); he mentioned what punishment would be inflicted on anyone who violated family or economic rules. He spelt out the rules that should be maintained between Muslims and non-Muslims, and how to deal with one another during the peaceful and war periods. In all of these, the all-embracing laws of Islam were carried out by Muhammad to set an example to his followers. These precedents were of great value for the succeeding generations of Muslims in demonstrating how Islamic laws, as prescribed in the *Qur'an*, were to be applied to different situations in Medina.

During this period, God and Muhammad were the sole legislators. God would reveal a law, and Muhammad would explain it and add to it what was necessary. The laws were introduced gradually to ease their acceptance and application. Some rules were modified, generalized or particularized by Muhammad when necessary. However, most of the laws in the *Qur'an* were revealed as responses to the questions that the believers asked.[10] The Prophet Muhammad in this period outlined the principles of actions relating to the rights of God and the rights of human beings.[11] He laid down major principles of law, which were flexible enough to accommodate the changing needs of time. The details of these laws were later spelled out and fully elaborated by his immediate disciples and scholars of the succeeding generations.[12] With the death of the Prophet Muhammad in 632 CE, the revelations ceased. Muslims were left to themselves to apply the law as they understood it. They believed that the religion of Islam had been completed; whatever was important to know about Islam had been taught to them by the Prophet. His death marked the end of God's revelations to human beings according to Islamic belief. Muslims believe that there would be no messenger of God after Muhammad.

> This day have I perfected your religion for you, completed My favor upon you, and have chosen for you Islam as your religion. (*Qur'an* 5:3)

The Period of the Companions (*Sahabah*) of the Prophet (632–661 CE)

Islam flourished after the death of Muhammad. It spread across the Arabian Peninsula. As many people began conversion to Islam, new issues emerged. Consequently, Muslims encountered new problems. At this time the immediate followers of Muhammad were the leaders of the Muslims. Whenever any legal issue appeared, they looked to the *Qur'an* for guidance. If they found a solution therein, they applied it. If not, they searched the traditions of the Prophet Muhammad for guidance, and if they found a solution, they applied it. When both the *Qur'an* and the *Sunnah* were silent on a novel issue, they assembled, consulted with one another and discussed the issue collectively. They decided what modification could be introduced, if necessary. They discussed the issue until they came to a unanimous opinion (*Ijma'*). Whatever conclusion they reached, they endorsed it and applied it.

The *Qur'an*, the *Sunnah* and the spirit of Islam guided these caliphs in their deliberations about legal issues. They considered themselves the bearers of the message of Islam. Wherever there was a need, they attended to it. At times they modified the *Sunnah* of the Prophet, which they had been privileged to witness. For instance, when the Prophet Muhammad was alive, the *Qur'an* set the punishment for illegal intercourse by an unmarried person with the opposite sex to be 100 lashes.[13] Then the Prophet added that such a person should be exiled for a year so that they would not be humiliated and looked upon with contempt in the community and so that they would not spread their immoral attitude in the society. During the reign of 'Umar bin Khattab, the second caliph, someone called Ibn Sar was convicted of fornication. He was punished and exiled to another city. Consequently, Ibn Sar converted to Christianity and abandoned Islam. 'Umar was informed of the situation. He called his advisors and sought their advice about what to do. Eventually they agreed that the punishment of exiling a criminal should be abolished because it did not serve the purpose for which it was established.[14] The reign of 'Umar bin al-Khattab witnessed a lot of changes and modifications to the legal system of Islam. The companions resorted to different methods, particularly *ijtihad* (exerting personal effort) and *Qiyas* (analogy), to align the law to the changing times and to the needs of the Muslim community. When they disagreed on an issue, as a result of different interpretations, they followed the views of the majority. Nevertheless, they were always motivated by the spirit of Islam. They tried their best to see that Islamic law was put on a solid legal foundation as it catered to the needs of the community.

The Period of Documentation and Establishment of Legal Theories (661–1258 CE)

Islamic law went through another stage of development when Mu'awiyyah became the leader of the Muslim Caliphate in 661 CE. Caliph Mu'awiyyah turned the Muslim community into an empire with its headquarters in Damascus, Syria. During this period, Muslim scholars initiated the transmission of the Hadith of the Prophet Muhammad. The companions of the Prophet were scattered across different cities of the empire. Whenever a problem occurred, the scholars in the locale would be consulted for advice. Each region had different solutions to the same problem owing to their different opinions: there was no unity. Some Muslims in Baghdad, Iraq, did not recognize the central government in Damascus. Those who followed Mu'awiyyah narrated many Hadith in support of whatever the Umayyad Caliphate was doing. Those who went against the caliphate, the Alids, the followers of Ali, narrated different reports from the Prophet. Each group claimed to possess the true traditions, which represented the true message of Islam.

Islamic law suffered tremendously during this period. The collection of the Hadith began and both genuine and spurious Hadith were disseminated among scholars. Umayyad Caliphs had the chance to do whatever they wanted, and at times they only paid lip service to the true application of the Islamic law. The rules, which were followed by the companions of the Prophet Muhammad, were not fully followed by the Umayyad's leaders. They established their own rules and applied them in whatever way they decided. The caliphs thus became the legislators. They introduced secular laws based on the customs of the Arabs, relying on the principles of personal judgment (*ijtihad)* rather than the laws established in the *Qur'an*. As a result, some scholars, such as Imam Shafi'i, argued vigorously that the sources of Islamic law should be based on the revealed text, the *Qur'an* and the *Sunnah*. He limited the understanding of the Hadith to only what is attributed to the Prophet Muhammad and not to the customs of the Arabs (*Sunnah*). He disproved the validity of the actions of the people of Medina (*'amal ahl al-madinah*), which Imam Malik considered authoritative, arguing that those actions could be wrong. He also disagreed with the school of Kufa, which relied heavily on personal reasoning (*Ra'y*) to determine the rules of law. Islamic law, Imam Shafi'i argued strongly, should be based on the text or its derivatives, not on personal reasoning, which is fraught with human desires and weaknesses.

Imam Shafi`i won recognition for the Hadith of the Prophet as the second source of Islamic law. The Umayyad Caliphs used this period of debate among the scholars to enact and apply whatever laws they wanted. They were far more inclined toward this world than to spiritual or religious issues. Their personal interests and secular considerations influenced their decisions and policies. At the same time, this period witnessed the beginning of the compilation of the traditions of the Prophet. Muslim scholars began to write books on Hadith and on the interpretations of the *Qur'an*. Subsequently, scholars from different locations emerged and different schools of law were born in different cities.

When the Abbasids took over the Islamic world around 750 CE, in their early period, they displayed more interests in relating their policies to Islamic norms to win people's hearts. The early schools of law developed and different disciplines of Islamic sciences were launched and supported by the Abbasid Caliphs Muslim scholars began to write classical books on Hadith, exegesis (*Tafsir*) and Islamic law. They paid great attention to education and to all sciences in general. Scholars debated and discussed with other scholars to defend their theories and their positions. There was tolerance and accommodation of opposing views. Hence the Islamic sciences were developed, nourished and patronized by kings and princes.

Unfortunately, this period of development did not last long. Muslim scholars began to divide themselves into different groups, sects and schools of thought. Each group began to think that it was the best. The generations that followed, from around 850 CE to 1258 CE, thought that what the scholars had accomplished was the apex of development. They believed that the ideas, theories and solutions suggested by them during this period were the final solutions for all Islamic legal problems, and thus they thought that those theories and solutions should not be questioned.[15] That was the beginning of the decline of Islamic law in theory as well as in practice.

After this period, the Islamic central government began to lose its grip and power over its constituencies one by one. Many small states emerged, which weakened the strength of the central government in Damascus, in Egypt, in Spain and in Iraq. Consequently, the application of Islamic law suffered and the law became static in that there were no new developments. What had already been written was considered adequate to meet the legal needs of the community. The Muslim scholars endorsed the imitation of old ideas, old theories and old judgments. The Muslim kings began to disregard Islamic law while the jurists began to protect and preserve what was written and accomplished previously. They felt that there was no need to develop new theories or generate new ideas and philosophies if the government was not ready to apply them.

The Period Between 1258–1900

This period witnessed a great decline in the Muslim world. The Ottoman Empire became the leaders of most of the Muslim world and codified Islamic law. However, its application of Islamic law was limited to those countries under Ottoman Empire. Other countries like India, West and North Africa were not under Ottoman's rule and thus these countries established their own Islamic legal systems and followed them. There was no central government for the whole Muslim world then.

The Period Between 1900–Present

This period the Western influence dominated most Muslim countries through colonization. Western laws were introduced into the Muslim world and some countries, such as Turkey, graciously embraced them and rejected

Islamic law, arguing that Islamic law was old and archaic. Thus Western law replaced Islamic law publicly and officially, and the only area left to the jurisdiction of Islam and to the Muslim judges was that of family law (*al ahwal al-shakhsiyyah*), which was also invaded during the middle of the twentieth century. Since the 1950s several Muslim reformers have called for the reapplication and re-establishment of Islamic law in Muslim countries. Many attempts have been made but no real success has been achieved owing to the alien force, the Western codified law, which has had its grip on and challenged the Muslim legal system. Muslim scholars in many parts of the world today are calling for the re-establishment and reapplication of Islamic law. Some countries, such as Iran, Yemen, Saudi Arabia, Sudan, Nigeria and Malaysia, have already begun incorporating some Islamic laws into their present legal systems. To what extent these laws will solve the legal problems of the Muslims in those countries is yet to be seen. However, Western law has never served the needs of Muslims because it ignores Muslim customs, religion and ways of life. Hence Muslims perceive Western law as alien, which they believe will not bring peace and stability to their communities.

The Sunni Schools of Law and Their Founders

As Islam spread to different parts of the Arabian Peninsula, a number of notable scholars emerged. They interpreted the laws of God differently owing to their varied understanding of the *Qur'an* and the environments in which they lived. In an attempt to apply the law of God, which they believed to be universal, they took into consideration the conditions of their locality, the interests of their audience and the amount of Islamic knowledge available to them. When the city of Medina was the capital and the only center of Islamic knowledge, during the reigns of Abu Bakr, Umar and Uthman, there was unanimous agreement on many legal problems. However, when the fourth caliph, Ali bin Abi Talib, moved the capital to Iraq, things began to change. When the Umayyad Empire chose Damascus as its headquarters, the center of Islamic knowledge was no longer restricted to Medina but was spread to Kufa and Damascus, as a result of the migration of some of the knowledgeable companions of the Prophet to those areas to assist the caliphs.

Eventually, new interpretations of the religion of Islam spread. Each locality felt free to abide by the decisions of its local scholars, and thus different schools of law came into existence which, for one reason or another, leaned toward specific methods of interpretation and application. They kept in mind the needs of their society. The emergence of these schools could be attributed to the flexibility of the principles of the law (*Shari`ah*), which allow it to be made suitable and applicable to different people in different places. The Muslim scholars, who developed these principles of law, did not claim any finality for their opinions or solutions. Rather, they thought that the legal decisions that they made were simply the best solutions for their society at that particular time.

In the third century of Islam (ninth century CE), there were many different schools of law that emerged. Only a few of them are in existence today. These include the four Sunni schools and the Shi'ite schools of law. The Sunni schools are the Hanafi, the Maliki, the Shafi'i and the Hanbali schools. Major schools of law among the Shi'ites are the Ja'afari school known as the Ithna-Ash'aris (the twelvers), the Zaydiyyah school and the Isma`ili schools. I will limit myself in this discussion to the Sunni schools. It should be pointed out that these four are similar in their approach to the law: one observes hardly any major differences among them in the real application of the law. They follow the same principles, particularly in regard to the *Qur'an*, the *Sunnah*, the *Ijma'* (consensus) and the *Qiyas* (analogy). The followers of each school vigorously attempt to distinguish themselves from one another, which has sometimes led to confrontation.

The Hanafi School and Its Founder, Imam Abu Hanifah

The Hanafi school is said to have been founded by Abu Hanifah, Thabit bin Nu'man bin Zuta. He was born in Iraq in 81 AH/700 CE.[16] There he grew up and received his knowledge from the local scholars before he traveled to Hijaz and learned about the science of Hadith from the renowned scholars at Medina. Thus he was well versed in Hadith contrary to the alleged claim that he had little knowledge of them.[17] Abu Hanifah was recognized as a great jurist or the father of Islamic law with an in-depth knowledge of the traditions of the Prophet and his companions. Since he was also a trader, he did not work for the government. Thus he was able to express his legal opinions without any fear of the established government in Iraq. Abu Hanifah was well known for his piety, generosity, kindness and asceticism. He had many students, who documented his methods of interpreting the law and his principles of jurisprudence. It was said that Abu Hanifah was the first scholar in Islam to introduce systematic legal thought, and a process of deducing the legal principles from the text and applying those rules to the practical matters of human life; he made use of reason and analogy to expand them.[18] Wherever the expressed law fails to serve its purpose, he applied the law of equity (*istihsan*), relying on the spirit of Islam. To him, the *Shari`ah's* objective is to bring peace and justice into the society.

Abu Hanifa's principles of jurisprudence can be summarized as follows. First, he considered the *Qur'an* to be the primary source of Islamic law. If he found no answer in it, he looked into the *Sunnah* of the Prophet; if he found no solution, he investigated the opinions of the companions of the Prophet and chose whatever he considered best suited the situation. In this he used his own method of verifying the transmission and reliability of the *Sunnah*. He accepted only the authentic tradition. He was very strict in his selection of the *Sunnah*. In the absence of any opinion among the companions, he formed his own opinion based on his personal reasoning, *ijtihad*.[19] He would not follow the views of the successors (the *tabi'un*); he considered himself to be equal to them. Abu Hanifah was credited as having introduced the law of equity (*istihsan*) into the legal system of Islam. This legal principle (*istihsan*) was criticized by some Muslim jurists, particularly Imam Shafi`i, on the grounds that its scope cannot be finely defined. *Istihsan*, Imam Shafi'i argues, is a guess and an arbitrary form of legal reasoning; the law of God should not be based on conjecture or on non-textual supported principle.[20] Abu Hanifah disagreed.

It is not certain whether Imam Abu Hanifah himself wrote any books. Certainly his students wrote many, which they attributed to him. His school is known as the Hanafi School and it spread all over the Muslim world, especially in India, Pakistan and Afghanistan. It tends to rely more on Qur'anic texts and Prophetic traditions. It also pays great attention to human reasoning in interpreting, deducting and applying the laws of God. The *Qur'an,* the authentic *Sunnah* and reasoning (*ra'y*), the school argues, complement one another.

The Maliki School of Law and Its Founder, Imam Malik

The Maliki school of law is known as School of Hijaz. It was in Medina that the Prophet Muhammad received most of the revelations of the *Qur'an*. Medina became the center of knowledge of the traditions of the Prophet. Many Muslims from all over the Muslim countries often visit Medina during the yearly pilgrimage. Many scholars and students stay afterwards to learn from the renowned scholars of Medina. It was in this city that Imam Malik Ibn Anas, al-Asbahi was born. His exact birthday is disputable.[21] He grew up and received his education there. He studied under different renowned scholars and never traveled out of the city except to Mecca during the pilgrimage. Imam Malik was an accomplished man of learning who brought great fame to Medina. He taught many students, including Imam Shafi'i, the master architect of the Islamic jurisprudence, who believed strongly that any transmission of Hadith from Imam Malik was always authentic. Imam Malik was a pious and courageous person; he always expressed his opinions on legal issues without any fear of the authorities, even if his words were in danger of bringing some harm to him or subjecting him to persecution by the Umayyad Caliphs in Medina.

Like his predecessors and contemporaries in Medina, Imam Malik did not develop what is known today as a theory of law. Primarily, he recognized the *Shari`ah* as a divine law with two principal aims: to strengthen one's relationship with God and to establish justice among human beings. All laws should be located in the *Qur'an* and in the explanatory examples of the Prophet Muhammad, the *Sunnah*. When Imam Malik could not find provision for a case in these two sources, he resorted to other sources for guidance. He endorsed, as a source of law, the practice of the people of Medina (*amal ahl al-Madinah*),[22] analogy (*qiyas*), a one-man narrated Hadith (*khabar al-Wahid*)[23] and the consideration of the common good of the people (*maslahah mursalah*).

Although he paid great attention to the Hadith of the Prophet, he was also very critical of Hadith literature. He verified a Hadith to determine its authenticity and genuineness before he accepted it. His students suggested some reasons why he accepted or rejected a Hadith; they found him to be systematic and consistent in his approach. His legal theories were inferred from the books that were attributed to him. At times he made implicit statements to express a preference for a certain source. His acceptance of the practice of the people of Medina and the recognition of the concept of public interest (*maslahah*) as legal theory has received sharp criticism from one of his students, Imam Shafi`i, who disagreed with him completely. Imam Shafi'i argued that the practice of the people of Medina should not override an expressed *Sunnah* of the Prophet. The response of the Maliki school is that if the oral tradition was authentic, the companions of the Prophet would be the first people to practice it. That is, if any tradition was not practiced, then it indicated that the Prophet did not say it or introduce it. Imam Shafi'i also argued that the concept of *maslahah* cannot be regulated because it is based on the desire of the Muslim scholars. He contended that what is considered to be good for one community may not be good for another. The law, he insisted, should not be based on a theory that cannot be measured or regulated.

Despite all of this criticism, it is agreed that Imam Malik wrote a book on Hadith, which became an authentic source and a classic text on Muslim traditions and jurisprudence. This work is known as *al-muwatta,* the trodden path. It was arranged according to the topics in jurisprudence. Imam Malik spent many years writing this book and continuously revising it until he died. The Abbasid caliphs, al-Mansur and Haruna al-Rashid, wanted to endorse the use of *al-Muwatta* at the Islamic courts throughout the Abassid Empire, but Imam Malik objected to such enforcement, arguing that there are more Islamic traditions than those that he included in his book, and therefore no one should be forced to use his book. Imam Shafi'i claimed that *al-Muwatta* is the most authentic book after the *Qur'an*. Perhaps that assessment could only be made prior to the compilation of many other authentic books about Hadith, like those of Imam al-Bukhari and Imam Muslim.

Imam Malik died in 179 AH/795 CE, leaving behind his *al-Muwatta* and some other books on Hadith, which were attributed to him by his students. The Maliki school was named after him. It spread all over the Muslim world: North Africa, West Africa and Upper Egypt. His *al-Muwatta* has been used in many *Shari`ah* courts as a source book of Islamic law. It has been translated into many languages too.

The Shafi'i School of Law and Its Founder, Imam Shafi'i

The Shafi'i school of law represents the middle path between the Hanafi school, which leans more on reasoning (*ra'y*), and the Maliki school, which gives more attention to the traditions of the Prophet. The Shafi'i school has been considered the most structured in that Imam Shafi'i worked out, in concrete terms, the principles and the sources on which Islamic law should be based. It was founded by Imam Shafi'i, Muhammad bin Idris al-Qurashi. He was born in Gaza in 150 AH/767 CE, the year when Imam Abu Hanifah died. He was first educated by his mother and received his knowledge in Hijaz before he traveled to Kufa in Syria, and Egypt. From his youth he showed a keen interest in learning. On his visit to Medina he became a student of Imam Malik and accompanied him until he died. He then went to Baghdad in Iraq, where he studied under Muhammad Ibn Hasan al-Shaybani, a student of Imam Abu Hanifah. By so doing, he acquired the knowledge of the scholars of Iraq and Hijaz, weaved them together and established his own school of law. This gave him a prominent position among the Muslim jurists of the time.

Imam Shafi`i is recognized as the master architect of Islamic jurisprudence in that he was able to write down, systematically, the sources he relied on in interpreting, deducing and applying Islamic law. As he was well versed in the Arabic language, he used that knowledge to explicate the direct and indirect meanings of the *Qur'an* and to formulate the principles of the science of abrogation and abrogated verse. He debated thoroughly with his contemporary scholars until the Hadith was recognized as the second source of Islamic law, and he gave a new meaning to the idea of the Hadith. He insisted that the Hadith should be limited to what Muhammad said, did and approved. He affirmed that both the *Qur'an* and the Hadith are the only primary sources of Islam; all other sources, he argued, are secondary and should not be accorded the same value. Although Imam Shafi`i recognized the consensus of the companions and the analogy as sources of Islamic law, he disagreed to some extent with the consensus of the people of Medina. He stated that the deeds of those people did not represent the views of all scholars in that city. He also disapproved of the way in which Iraqi scholars used analogy (*qiyas*) and the concept of equity (*Istihsan*). He considered *Istihsan* a guess and an arbitrary judgment, which had no strong foundation, thus *Istihsan* should not be used as a source of law, in his opinion. The Hanafis disagreed with this. To them, *Istihsan* is a means of correcting the mistakes of the law, especially when its application fails to achieve its objective.

Imam Shafi'i accorded great respect to his teacher, Imam Malik, yet he disagreed with him on several occasions, particularly regarding the concept of *maslahah mursalah*, the consideration of the public good. He argued that only God is the legislator. The law, he insisted, is only that which is expressed in the *Qur'an* or derived from it. Human's duties are to understand the law and apply it to their daily life; they should not become legislators. He debated with his opponents and wrote his historical book, *A Treatise on the Principle of Islamic Jurisprudence* (*ar-Risalah*). Therein he elaborated his arguments, and responded forcefully and with clarity to those who opposed his views. Eventually he won many disciples and students, who included Imam Ahmad bin Hanbal, the founder of the Hanbali school of law, Daud al-Zahiri, the founder of the Zahirite school, and the literalists. Imam Shafi'i was claimed to have written many books. However, recent research has shown that his students wrote many of those attributed to him but faithfully followed his methodology.[24]

Fortunately for him, most of the early Islamic scholars, who compiled books on the traditions of the Prophet and on Islamic law, belonged to the

Shafi'i school, such as Imam al-Bukhari, Imam Muslim, al-Tirmizi, Ibn Majah, Abu Daud, Ibn Kathir, Abu Hamid al-Ghazali, al-Bayhaqi and al-Suyuti. The Shafi'i school spread all over the Muslim world. Imam Shafi'i frequently revised his views, so his opinions and verdicts have often been qualified as a first opinion or a latter opinion. The reason for this is that, when he was with Imam Malik, he was not fully exposed to the outside world beyond the Arabian Peninsula. When he visited Iraq and Egypt, his views changed owing to the reality of life and circumstances he encountered in those countries. Imam Shafi'i died in Cairo in 204 AH/819 CE and was buried there. He was quoted as having said that true knowledge is not that which is memorized but that which benefits the people. Today, Muslims in Indonesia, Malaysia and Egypt follow the Shafi'i school.

The Hanbali School of Law and Its Founder, Imam Ahmad Bin Hanbal

The Hanbali school is called neither the Hijazi school nor the Iraqi school, even though it leans towards the former in that Imam Ahmad, the founder, placed an emphasis on the traditions of the Prophet Muhammad more than on any other source of law other than the Qur'an. Imam Ahmad bin Hanbal was born in Baghdad, Iraq, in 164 AH/780 CE and he died there in 241AH/855 CE. He grew up in Baghdad, received his knowledge there and then traveled to many major Islamic places, such as Medina, Mecca, Kufa in Egypt, Yemen and Syria, in search of more knowledge. He was one of the outstanding students of Imam Shafi`i and he never left him until his teacher's death. It was reported that he respected Imam Shafi'i so much that he would never give any verdict (*fatwa*) when his elder was in Baghdad.

With regard to his legal theories, he leaned towards the supremacy of the tradition of the Prophet Muhammad (*Sunnah*) over any other source except for the *Qur'an*. He adhered strictly to the text of the *Qur'an* and the *Sunnah*. If he found no solution in the traditions, he resorted to the consensus of the scholars, particularly the verdicts (*fatawa*) of the companions, provided that there was nothing to contradict them. He did not wholeheartedly support analogy (*Qiyas*) as a source of law, although, at times, he used it. However, he preferred a Hadith reported by one person (*khabar al-wahid*) to analogy (*qiyas*). Owing to his heavy reliance on the Hadith, some scholars, such as Ibn 'Abd al-Barr and al-Tabari, did not consider him to be a jurist. They recognized him as a *muhaddith* (one versed in the Hadith traditions).

Imam Ahmad was renowned for his works, particularly his compilation of the traditions of the Prophet, the *Musnad*. This work was arranged according to the names of the narrators. That is, Imam Ahmad reported all Hadith that were reported by each single narrator from the Prophet. He did not follow the method of the jurists of arranging the Hadith according to the legal topics, as did Imam Malik. It was reported that Imam Ahmad memorized more than 100,000 Hadith and wrote down only 40,000, which he rated as authentic. Many scholars argued that Imam Ahmad's collection includes some Hadith that are weak compared with the collections of Imam al-Bukhari or Imam Muslim. However, Imam Ahmad was known to be pious, dedicated and firm in his faith. He was imprisoned and tortured for twenty-eight months by one of the Abbasid Caliphs, al-Mu'tasim, because of his views about the *Qur'an*. He gained great fame for his insistence on the uncreatedness[25] of the *Qur'an* and his steadfastness in the face of persecution. That period is known in Muslim history as the period of inquisition (*mihnah*), whereby all those scholars who did not subscribe to the rationalists' (Mu'tazilite) opinions were punished by the government. The Hanbali school is followed predominantly in present-day Saudi Arabia and by some Muslims in Syria, Palestine and Iraq. It is the least widespread of the four Sunni schools. Many Muslims in Africa have never heard of the Hanbali school until they travel on pilgrimage to Saudi Arabia.

Towards the end of nineteenth and the beginning of twentieth century, Muslim countries fell under colonial rule by Western countries. West Africa in particular fell under British and French rule. It did not win back its independence until 1960s. During the occupation, the colonial rulers changed the culture of the West African peoples and introduced their own languages. They enacted new laws and wrote new constitutions for them. Where there were existing Islamic laws, such as in Northern Nigeria and Senegal, the colonial rulers replaced them with European laws or modified them to the extent that they no longer reflected Islamic law. The only area which the colonial rulers did not tamper with completely was "personal laws," known as *al-ahwal al-shakhsiyyah*. These covered only family law. Nevertheless, they continuously criticizing the remaining family law until many Muslim countries modified it to resemble European law, as evidenced in North Africa: Egypt, Tunisia, Algeria and Morocco. Today the so-called Islamic law in many Muslim countries is modified European law;[26] it does not represent classic Islamic law. Thus Islamic movements have emerged in all of these countries, calling for the re-establishment of Islamic law and the repeal of the existing law, which is deemed foreign to the people and unrepresentative of their religious and cultural life.

Unfortunately, the application of Islamic law has occasionally been abused by Muslims, especially regarding capital punishment and criminal laws (the *Hudud* laws). These abuses have occurred in nearly all Muslim countries to the extent that the people have objected to this application. They cite the bad experience and abuse of Islamic law by the Taliban in Afghanistan, Pakistan, Sudan and Nigeria, as well as by ISIS in Iraq currently. In all of these countries, women have been abused and discriminated against, and they do not receive equitable justice in the Islamic courts in these countries. They do not receive any civil or social rights from their government. Hence they become subjects of oppression and persecution. Often women do not receive adequate education from the public schools. In some areas, they are not allowed to attend schools for the fear that they might be molested. When women commit any wrong, they may receive severe punishment in comparison to men who commit similar crimes, as evidenced in the case of Safiya and Amina Lawal in Nigeria who were charged with adultery.[27]

However, it should be pointed out that the Afghanistan regime under the Taliban's government was practicing extreme Islamic criminal laws (*hudud*) which did not represent the spirit of Islam as pointed out by many of today's scholars of Islam. Nevertheless, the majority of Muslims would still prefer to be judged by Islamic law, which they believe is part of their religion. Even though some Muslims may not want *Shari`ah* law to be the only legal system in their country, they do not wish to discard it. Where the citizens have the freedom to choose between common law and *Shari`ah* law, the majority would choose the *Shari`ah*, as seen in Northern Nigeria, Iraq and other countries in North Africa. Statistics have shown that in Northern Nigeria, *Shari`ah* courts adjudicate more cases than other State courts. Many citizens prefer to take their cases to the *Shari`ah* courts because of the trust they have in them. The only exception is with criminal cases, the majority of which ended up at magistrates' courts.

Notes

1. Lord Lugard was the governor of Nigeria appointed by the British Empire. He conquered Northern Nigeria in 1903.
2. For more information about the early history of Nigeria, see Crowder, Michael Ajayi. *A Short History of Nigeria*. New York: Frederich A. Praeger, 1966.

3. The population of each religious group in Nigeria is controversial because each group inflates the number of its adherents for political purposes. Therefore the numbers change occasionally. The idea that Christianity has the largest number of followers among the Yoruba is always contested by the Yoruba Muslims, who claim that their population is greater. What is known for sure is that there are more Muslims than Christians in Nigeria, and that indigenous religion is losing followers as a result of modern education and aggressive work by both Muslim and Christian missionaries.
4. For more information about politics in the early history of Nigeria before and after independence, see Schwarz, Frederick A. O. *Nigeria: The Tribes, The Nation, or the Race—The Politics of Independence.* (Cambridge, MA. MIT Press, 1965).
5. For more information about education in Nigeria, see World Education News and Reviews, "Education in Nigeria" published on July 1, 2013. Access at: www.wenr.wes.org on June 12, 2015.
6. Owhonda, John. *Nigeria: A Nation of Many Peoples.* New Jersey, Parsippany: Dillon Press, 1998.
7. For more information about Nigeria and Yoruba cultures in Nigeria, see Lawal, Nike S, Sadiku, Matthew N. O, Dopamu, Ade. *Understanding Yoruba Life and Culture.* N.J., Trenton: Africa World Press Inc., 2004.
8. Cyril Glasse, *The Concise Encyclopedia of Islam* (San Francisco: Harper & Row, Publishers, Inc., 1989), p. 361.
9. Sobhi M. Mahmassani, *Falsafat al-Tashri fi al-Islam* [The Philosophy of Jurisprudence in Islam] (Leiden: E.J. Brill, 1961), p. 10.
10. There are many examples of this in the *Qur'an*. For instance, someone came to Muhammad and asked whether he could marry an idol worshipper. The answer came that he could not, as stated in the *Qur'an* ch 2:221. Another person came and asked whether he should write down a contract if he borrowed from another. The answer came that he should write any contract down, as stated in ch 2:282.
11. Whenever Muslim scholars label anything as the rights of God (*huquq Allah*), they are referring to the public rights.
12. Anwar A. Qadri, *Islamic Jurisprudence in the Modern World* (Pakistan, Lahore: Sh. Muhammad Ashraf, 1981, pp. 43–49.
13. "The woman and the man guilty of adultery or fornication, flog each of them with a hundred stripes. Let not compassion moves you in their case, in a matter prescribed by God, if you believe in God and the last day; and let a party of the believers witness their punishment" (*Qur'an* 24:2).
14. They also argued that sending a criminal to another town or community would be wrong because he might spread his crime there too since he would be a stranger in a place where many people would be unaware of his past criminal record. Today we have seen child molesters and rapists separated from the community.

15. For more information about the history of the development of Islamic law, see Kemal A. Faruki, *Islamic Jurisprudence* (Pakistan, Lahore: National Book Foundation, 1975), pp. 20–33.
16. AH refers to the Islamic calendar, which is a lunar calendar.
17. Noah Ha Him Keller, *The Reliance of the Traveller*, trans. of *Umdat al-Salik* (Il, Evenaston: Sunna Books, p. 1027.
18. Mahmassani, pp. 19–21.
19. Mahmassani, p. 20, quoting Ibn `Abd al-Barr, *Al-Intiqa' fi Fada'ili ath-Thalathah*, p. 143.
20. Hallaq, *A History of Islamic Legal Theories*, p. 108.
21. Some reports put his birth at 95, 96 or 98 AH/713, 715 or 716 CE. It was agreed that he died in 179 AH/795 CE.
22. The principle of accepting the practice of the people of Medina means that when an act is practiced by those people, it has more validity than oral tradition, which is not practiced. Action speaks loud, Imam Malik would argue.
23. *Khabar al wahid* is a report which the narrator attributed to the Prophet Muhammad. Only one narrator claimed to have heard it from the Prophet. The question which the scholars of Hadith are asking is, if the Prophet Muhammad said it, why should it not be heard or reported by other companions?
24. For more information about Imam Shafi`i and his methodology in Islamic jurisprudence, see Al-Imam Muhammad ibn Idris al-Shafi'i, *Al-Risala fi Usul al-Fiqh* [Treatise on the Foundations of Islamic Jurisprudence], translated with an introduction, notes and appendices by Majid Khadduri, 2ed. Cambridge: The Islamic Texts Society, 1987.
25. This means that the *Qur'an* is not a creation but the words of God revealed to Muhammad within a period of twenty-three years.
26. In Tunisia, Morocco and Algeria, most of the family laws have been modified; these countries banned polygamous marriage and insisted that male and female heirs receive equal shares from the properties left by the deceased. The *Qur'an* stipulates that men get two-thirds while women get just a third.
27. The case of Amina Lawal and Safiya is fully analyzed in Chapter 4?

CHAPTER 2

A History of Islamic Law in Nigeria

Introduction: A History of Islam in Nigeria Before the Advent of the *Jihad*

The history of the introduction of the application of Islamic law in Nigeria cannot be separated from the advent of Islam itself in what is known today as Northern Nigeria. Islam first arrived in Africa in 615 CE when Muhammad, the Prophet of Islam, sought refuge with the Christian king (King Negus-Najashi) of Ethiopia (formerly Abyssinia).[1] Muhammad sent his disciples there to escape social and racial persecution in Mecca. King Negus received the Muslims warmly and accorded them great respect. He allowed them to stay and to practice their religion as long as they wanted. He provided them with security, and the Muslims stayed there until Muhammad migrated to Medina and established the Islamic state. Thus many Africans were exposed to Islam at this time, and since then Islam has remained in Africa in one form or another.

This section focuses on the introduction of Islam to Nigeria and the role the Fulani leaders played in spreading Islam and its law. The discussion includes how Islamic law was applied before and during British colonial rule in Nigeria, as well as before and after Nigerian independence in 1960. We shall concentrate on Northern Nigeria, where Islamic law has operated. It is pertinent to mention here that Islamic law gained a foothold in the north in the nineteenth century because of the indirect rule adopted by Lord Lugard (the appointed British governor for all of Northern Nigeria) when he conquered Sokoto in 1903.

Y. Sodiq, *A History of the Application of Islamic Law in Nigeria*,
DOI 10.1007/978-3-319-50600-5_2

Nigeria, more particularly Northern Nigeria, enjoys considerable fame in connection with what is called "indirect rule" or, as the latest refinement has it, "indirect administration."[2] Indirect rule entailed that the native people who were in power before the conquest would remain in their posts, and the emirs who were exercising power previously would be responsible for the administration of their people, while the Britons would supervise their activities and provide administrative advice where needed.

Further, most of the country was already under the control of the Fulani emirates. Sir Fredrick Lugard was impressed by the quality of their administrative machinery and ability. He did the obvious, indeed the inevitable: he left the emirates to continue as they were, subject only to certain broad limitations.[3]

Owing to this indirect rule policy, the colonial regime imposed restrictions on the movement of missionaries in the protectorates where the policy was in operation.[4] This in effect gave ample opportunity for Islamic law, at least, to retain its domination and applicability in the north even today. There was no time in the history of the colonial period when Islamic law was completely abandoned or outlawed. However, it suffered a considerable setback during the British occupation, especially regarding criminal law.

It should be noted that the spread of Islam in Northern Nigeria can also be attributed to the effort of the Muslim scholars who spread Arabic literacy before the invasion of the British and the adoption of Arabic script for the translation of some African languages into writing. These scholars also created Arabic alphabet letters for the vernacular languages, which, to a larger extent, contributed tremendously to the spread of Jihadist ideas and philosophies in West Africa.

Islam in the Kanem-Bornu Empire

Islam came to the country which today is known as Nigeria at different times and from different directions. No reference can be made to a particular time when the process of Islamization began in Nigeria, or to a specific factor that triggered it. Many sources assert that Islam had its earliest roots in the extreme northeast of Nigeria—that is, in the Bornu Empire between the seventh and eighth centuries.[5] The exact year is unknown, and it appears that only a few individuals embraced Islam during the early period. Islam in Nigeria witnessed its first development in the eleventh century when the state had its first Muslim ruler, Hummay in Kanem.[6]

Islam began gaining ground during the reign of Mai Idris Alooma, who attempted to establish Islamic law on a wide scale.[7] Hiskett mentions that Alooma opened many educational centers and had diplomatic links with other Muslim regions, such as Tripoli and Turkey.[8] He argues that, despite all his attempts to establish it, there is no convincing evidence that Islamic law was adopted as the state law, nor that Islam swept away non-Islamic beliefs and practices.[9] Islamic law was not chosen as the state law because the people were attached to their customs. Hogben[10] points out that some rulers[11] who became Muslims reverted at times to their native religions because of the cultural pressure exerted on them by their society. Nevertheless, attempts made by a number of *mai* [12] in Bornu Empire resulted in influencing and spreading Islamic culture in the region.

Brenner points out that although the state had not become fully Islamic, "the rulers had no choice but to appoint the Muslims as Imams, judges and their close advisors due to their literacy in Arabic language."[13] Thus by the sixteenth and seventeenth centuries, Islam appears to have played a significant role in the intellectual, cultural, political and religious life of the entire Kanem-Bornu Empire.[14] Clarke claims that this resulted from the increased number of Muslim scholars and their ascendance to key posts, which gave them political authority despite their small number compared with native religionists, who were unable to read or write. In addition, the records show that the kings employed some Muslim scholars as judges who in turn applied Islamic law wherever possible in many affairs of the state. Thus although Islamic law was not totally enforced and did not cause a radical transformation of the society, its influence on the people's lifestyle cannot be denied.[15]

From this short history it can be seen that the application of Islamic law in the Bornu Empire was minimal. It was present only in those areas where the rulers allowed it to operate. The duties assigned to the Muslim scholars might include the performance of daily prayers, maintenance of mosques and running of schools, which were established by local teachers, performing marriage contracts between Muslim men and women, and officiating at naming ceremonies and religious funeral services.

The judges exercised and discharged their duties as required by the kings. In fact, Muslim judges could not go against the interests of the rulers who appointed them, so Islamic law was applied only when it served the interests of the rulers.[16] Two reasons may be given for the attitude of Muslims: they recognized, through their knowledge or experience, that living with non-Muslims without opposing their ways of life and by not imposing Islamic law on them would help to prepare the people to accommodate Muslims;

or they had little knowledge of Islamic law, Islamic science and Islamic history, which limited their influence and effect on the society.

A third reason why Muslim scholars might not have opted for full application of Islamic law was the fear of losing their political positions, which they won only because of their literacy. Therefore they compromised with non-Muslims and developed the attitude of tolerance, which the situation forced on them. Whether they were satisfied with that situation cannot be easily determined. Nevertheless, the warm reception offered by the indigenous people to the Muslim traders on their first arrival in Nigeria prevented the Muslims from developing a militant attitude against their hosts. The Muslims saw the natives as friends and co-religionists, even though they worshipped different gods.

Islam in Hausa Land

It is uncertain exactly when Islam came to Hausa land.[17] Some historians ascribed the advent of Islam there to the eleventh and fourteenth centuries.[18] Islam spread gradually until some of the Hausa rulers, such as Muhammad Rumfa (1463–1499 AD),[19] became Muslim. During Rumfa's reign, Muslims increased in number, and he made an effort to standardize Islam as the state religion. One of his attempts was his invitation to Shaykh Muhammad 'Abd al-Kareem al-Maghili from Morocco to visit Kano.[20] Shaykh al-Maghili arrived and found that Islam had little effect on the daily life of the people. Reportedly, he embarked on educational reforms by establishing new schools, strengthening the existing ones and appointing judges to various posts after getting the approval of the local rulers.

After winning the support of the natives, al-Maghili appealed to the rulers to apply Islamic law in their empires.[21] Because of his scholarship, he was asked by Rumfa to write a treatise on the administration of justice. He wrote a treatise entitled "Obligations of the Princes."[22] In it he explained that the major duty of a ruler was to improve the faith and welfare of the people, and that the ruler should not become the master over the people but their servant.[23] His activities in Hausa land attracted many students to Kano.

Muhammad al-Maghili witnessed much change and progress, especially in the furthering of Islamic education and the reformation of the judicial system. He became a judge at Katsina and influenced the appointment of some of his students as judges both there and in Kano.[24] Although Islam found a good foothold in Hausa land, and many Hausa rulers from the fifteenth to the eighteenth centuries were Muslims and appointed Muslim scholars as judges, native laws were often resorted to.

Islamic Law Before the Sokoto Caliphate

The above discussion dealt with the coming of Islam to Hausa land before Shaykh Uthman Dan Fodio came on the scene. Development of the implementation of Islamic law had not really begun prior to the reforms introduced by Shaykh Uthman Dan Fodio. During the nineteenth century, he was regarded as the most articulate reformer of Islam in the whole of West Africa. He was born in Gobir in 1754 to Fulani parents whose ancestors were from Senegal. He studied traditional Islamic sciences in his youth under the tutelage of his relatives and with a number of learned men of the time. From his school days "he combined an exceptionally high moral character with great intellectual gifts and evolved into a man of vivid eloquence, which assisted him in his profession as a teacher and preacher." His preaching took him to various cities of Hausa land where he found, to his surprise, that Islamic law was not adhered to by the Hausa rulers. He recognized that many non-Islamic practices and social injustices prevailed in all parts of Hausa land.

Shaykh Uthman was displeased with the situation in which public institutions were not governed by Islamic principles. Therefore he determined to make a change. Recognizing that this wasn't possible without first educating and enlightening the people, he embarked on a large-scale educational program in which he taught all classes, including women, about Islam and its ethics. At first he avoided any confrontation with the rulers. However, as time went on, the rulers and Muslim scholars who had a great interest in maintaining the status quo conspired to "erect a thick wedge between the masses and the true Islamic teachings."[25] It was reported that they tried to curtail Islamization: they gave no support to the shaykh, who constantly asked them to mold their lives in an Islamic way and implement Islamic law so as to do justice and be fair to their people.

Unfortunately, the Habe rulers did not heed his advice or his preaching.[26] His appeal met stiff resistance from both political and religious leaders until tensions grew between the Muslim community represented by Shaykh Uthman and the rulers.[27] The latter resorted to their power and authority, boldly denouncing Islam and its adherents, as was evidenced in the king of Gobir's legislation, which was announced in all markets of the state. The ruler of Gobir announced:

1. It is illegal for anyone, apart from Shaykh Uthman Dan Fodio, to preach Islam to the people and admonish them.
2. None other than those born to Muslim families are allowed to practice Islam. All converts must, therefore, revert back to the religion of their ancestors, which are the traditional native religions.

3. No one is allowed to wear a turban, and no woman is allowed to cover her body according to the demands of the *Shari`ah*.[28]

As a result of this declaration and the attempt to assassinate him (as reports have shown), Shaykh Uthman called on his followers to prepare to defend themselves.[29] He ran from Degel to Gudu in defence of his faith.[30] At that point he charged the Hausa rulers with a number of corrupt practices, which, in his view, justified their removal from the throne because they were not serving the interests of their people. The most important among these charges were:

1. The Habe rulers imposed taxes that were non-Islamic, like the cattle tax (*jangali*).
2. They were accused of extortion.
3. They took bribes and failed to observe Islamic law on matters of inheritance and succession.
4. They coerced people to serve in their military force and punished those who failed to serve.

Shaykh Uthman also charged them with polytheistic practices, such as worshipping trees, stones, rocks and supernatural beings.[31] He accused the scholars who supported the kings of compromising their religion for material reward. For these allegations and the bitter denunciation of the Habe leaders and their associates, the Gobir leaders waged a war against the followers of Shaykh Uthman wherever they were. In response, Shaykh Uthman and his followers defended themselves. He also claimed that the purpose of his *Jihad* was "to make the word of God supreme" and to suppress the tyrannical rule of the Hausa.[32]

The tension between the Muslim community and the Hausa rulers reached a climax within a short period, leading to a confrontation on the battlefield in 1804. By the end of 1808, Shaykh Uthman and his followers were victorious. They established themselves as the new leaders of the Sokoto Caliphate,[33] claiming their purpose to be "commanding what is right and forbidding what is wrong."[34] Henceforth, they declared Shaykh Uthman to be the spiritual and political leader of the new state. To consolidate the empire, he made a number of reforms, among which was the legal system.

Application of *Shari`ah* Law During the Sokoto Caliphate

Immediately after the *Jihad*, Shaykh Uthman, his brother Abdullah ibn Fodio and Muhammad Bello (his son) worked hard to replace the existing legal system with an Islamic one. They recognized that establishing an Islamic legal system was one of the most important functions of the government. They embarked on reforming the existing courts and building new ones, and they retained the king's palaces as court rooms. Shaykh Uthman supplied them with capable scholars, knowledgeable in Islamic law, to be judges.[35] He appointed the judges himself[36] and assigned them duties.[37] The judges were to seek advice from him only. He also appointed police officers who executed punishment on the criminals. He selected Muezzin Muhammad Julde as the chief complaint officer (*Muhtasib*), who overlooked the conduct of the judges to see that they discharged their duties well and that the people involved were treated with fairness and justice. Three types of court were established during Shaykh Uthman's time: Alkali's court, Emir's courts and an appeal court. He headed the latter court himself.[38]

It is worth noting that Shaykh Uthman, in his work *Bayan Wujub al-Hijrah*, and Shaykh 'Abdullah Ibn Fodio, in *Diya' al-Hukkam*, were concerned about the administration of justice. They explained the qualifications of judges, the sources they should rely on in adjudication, and where and when they could resort to their own discretion (*Ijtihad*) in the absence of textual guidance from the *Qur'an* or the *Sunnah*.[39] They also emphasized the support needed from other sections of government, such as the public complaints office and police sections, to enforce the judgments of the judiciary. They insisted that, in an Islamic state, the weak should be able to obtain justice from the powerful through the administration of justice; and the powerful should be able to enjoy liberty of action as long as no harm is caused to others.

Many institutions, such as schools and correctional institutions, were established during Shaykh Uthman's lifetime. They were reinforced and restructured by Muhammad Bello, who was regarded as the master architect of the Sokoto Caliphate. Furthermore, during that caliphate, the principles of legislation rested on certain concepts adopted by Shaykh Uthman and his followers. These principles were seen as the bedrock of the state's policy in the administration of justice.[40] Shaykh Uthman laid them down to guide the judges in their daily assignments. He stipulated that in the sphere of legislation, only the *Qur'an* and the *Sunnah* are binding on Muslims. All other opinions represent the personal discretion of the scholars (*ulama*) and are not binding.[41] Therefore law-enforcement agencies, judges and legislators should comply with the provisions of the *Qur'an* and the *Sunnah* as much as possible. All views that not emanating directly from these sources should not be forced on the people, nor should the people be censured for not complying with them.

Shaykh Uthman had already emphasized this notion in his book *Ihya' al-Sunnah wa Ikhmad al-Bid'ah al-Shaytaniyyah*—that is, only action which is directly opposed to the *Qur'an* and the *Sunnah* can be condemned. All other practices that are not opposed to them should not be rejected, even if they do not conform with Maliki school's opinions.[42]

The other principle emphasized by Shaykh Uthman is that of tolerance and accommodation of opposing views (*al-tawfiq bayn al- 'ara'*).[43] According to him, this principle is embodied in the Islamic notion that differences of opinion among his people are a mercy from God. This means that free expression of opinion is permitted, so no one should repudiate another who holds a different view. It also implies that people should be given ample chance to express their opinions, which may or may not concur with the prevailing views of the majority or accord with the opinion of the authorities. The mercy mentioned by the Prophet means that a Muslim should have a number of options to choose from,[44] and by being given such a chance will find their solution in Islamic law. The implication is that a Muslim is not bound to follow one particular school of law. They can follow whichever school they prefer as long as they do so rationally. "All schools of law lead to Allah," claimed Shaykh Uthman.[45]

Another concept that he asserted as essential in the administration of justice was the notion that "religion is ease."[46] To him, the primary purpose of the law is to serve the people by lifting burdens off their backs, to allow the weak their rights, to improve the lot of the people, and to endow them with enough freedom to participate in the social, cultural and political affairs of their state. To him, justice prevails only when the scholars take a lenient approach to the law by adhering to its spirit rather than to its letter so that the law does not become "a tool of overcharging the people or straining their endurance."[47]

In addition, Shaykh Uthman argued that the application of Islamic law should be considered in the context of its usefulness to society. Therefore where there are two options, the administrators of Islamic law are supposed to choose the easier one, or even suspend application of any particular strict law for some time in favor of a more practicable policy, which may not conform to the letter of the law[48] but still serves the general purposes of Islam. There are many examples of this approach in Islamic legal systems.

In illustrating this point, Ibraheem Sulaiman[49] gives a vivid example in which Shaykh Uthman and Abdullah held different opinions.[50] When Uthman's followers left their residences to join him, they left all their property behind. This was confiscated by the Habe leaders. When the Muslims won, the original owners wanted their property back. Shaykh Uthman argued that any attempt to get back all that had been lost during the war would open up unending complaints, affect the morale of many followers and incite the non-believers to more violence. This would lead to further distortion of the goals of the *Jihad* and might even sow the germ of hatred and disunity among the believers. It might also divert the attention of the Sokoto leaders away from the reconstruction of the state that they had just begun. This process of overlooking what had occurred in the past was based on the notion of seeking that which is best (*maslahah*) for the state as a whole rather than running after individual interests. No doubt a fulfillment of the individual interest amounts to fulfillment of the goals of the public, but in this situation, argued Shaykh Uthman, the price that the state would pay for claiming the lost property would be the disunity of the state.

At the same time, Shaykh Uthman did not want to imprint on the minds of his followers that the *Jihad* was primarily fought to gain property from the rulers. Rather, he claimed that the aim of the war was to free them from the injustice of their oppressors by relieving their hardship and making life better. An easier and better life could only be achieved after the reconstruction and reshaping of the state in an Islamic way, he argued in his work *Najm al-Ikhwan*.[51] In contrast, Shaykh Abdullah saw no reason why the victorious Muslims could not reclaim their property.[52]

What can be drawn from the above example is that Shaykh Uthman promoted a notion of law that alleviates the suffering and hardship faced by the people. He also believed that in order to serve the people, it might at times be best not to adhere to the letter of the law, and that the principle of *maslahah* (public interest) must be given full consideration in any legislation.[53] This open approach to Islamic law provided Hausa people with a stable life and prosperity that they had not enjoyed before. As time went on, however, the later leaders of the Sokoto Caliphate, such as Sultan Attahiru I, applied the law strictly[54] and undermined the dynamism through which Shaykh Uthman, Abdullah, Bello and others governed the people. As a result, Islamic law suffered a setback at the advent of the British invasion of Northern Nigeria between 1901 and 1903 because of the adherence to the literal application of the law by the then leaders of the Sokoto Caliphate.

Critique of the Application of Islamic Law in the Sokoto Caliphate

There has been no study to prove the extent to which Islamic law was adhered to by the Sokoto Caliphate. Nevertheless, the amount of literature written by the Sokoto leaders[55] about how Islamic law should be applied, the establishment of the new courts and the appointment of new judges are a good indication that the state was governed mainly by Islamic law. Hence the spread of Islam, the stability of the state to some extent, and the spread of learning became noticeable. Freedom of movement within the areas dominated by Muslims might be ascribed to the application of Islamic law, which in corollary contributed to the progress attained by the Hausa people in a very short time.

Of course, those who were applying the law were seen to be very learned in Islamic law and had access to considerable libraries containing the works of eminent jurists in Islam. These books helped them to discharge their duties knowledgeably. However, this is not to say that there were no shortcomings in the application of Islamic law. There are reports that some practices which were condemned even by Shaykh Uthman before the *Jihad* were retained after it. Burns points out one example: the tax on cattle. This was regarded as unfair and unIslamic in the pre-*Jihad* campaign.[56] One would have thought that because it was condemned by Shaykh Uthman, it would have been abolished immediately after the state had declared itself Islamic, yet after the *Jihad* it was not abolished.[57] Its non-condemnation was based on the fact that the state needed money to implement its programs,

Equally disliked were the toll tax that the traders paid to Habe rulers at every town they passed.[58] This also was not initially abolished. In addition, one finds that the appeal of Shaykh Uthman to Muslims to use the concept of consultation (*shura*) when making policies was not strictly followed. One of the most important issues—the ascendance to the post of leadership or imamship—was hereditary in the Sokoto Caliphate.[59] Ascendance to posts by hereditary appointment is contrary to the normative teaching of Islam, which asserts that appointment or selection should be based on merit.[60] Muslim scholars today recommend that the most eligible person should be preferred.[61] There were some sultans, such as Atahiru I, who were perceived incompetent to be leaders, yet they held leadership posts in the Sokoto Caliphate on the basis of hereditary rule.[62]

Despite this critique, it is worth nothing that Shaykh Uthman was the only person in Islamic history who, after becoming the caliph through *Jihad*, left the leadership post and devoted the rest of his life to Islamic scholarship.[63] His attitude, in my view, refutes the assumption of some modern writers[64] that he fought the Hausa to uplift the Fulanis to the throne of Hausa leadership—that is, the *Jihad* was purely a racial war of the poor Fulanis, the cattle herders, against the Hausa bureaucrats, landlords, and merchants. However, there is too little evidence to prove this.

The changes that occurred after the *Jihad* showed that the struggle was not primarily for tribal purposes but for a complete reform of all aspects of life in Hausa land. Certainly some of Shaykh Uthman's military men were Hausas, and the Hausa language became the *lingua franca* of the people. Thus if the struggle was merely between the Fulanis and the Hausas, the Fulanis would have imposed their language as the state's language when they became victorious, but they did not.

In general, the application of *Shari`ah* in Northern Nigeria until 1900 may be divided into three stages: the early stage, between the eleventh and fourteenth centuries, when Islam was first introduced to Nigeria; the medieval stage, between the fifteenth and eighteenth centuries, when the Islamic religion was accepted by few natives and Islamic law was partially implemented; and the triumph stage, from 1808 until the end of the nineteenth century, when Islamic law was generally accepted as the law of the state.[65]

During the early stage, the assumption was that Muslims applied Islamic law in prayers, marriage contracts, burials and partially in the distribution of the estate of the deceased. According to Hasan Gwarzo,[66] there are no documented reports to substantiate this minimal application. He argues that these practices were the little things that could differentiate Muslims from non-Muslims during that period. He adds that the degree of application of those rules also depended largely on the amount of knowledge possessed by the Muslim scholars of the time. Burdon, however, alleges that although there were Muslim scholars and some of them were appointed as advisers to some kings, they were not practicing Islamic law. He says:

> At this time, [before Fulani *Jihad*] all the Hausa kings gave judgement arbitrarily without laws; learned Mallams were attached to them but they did what the kings ordered.[67]

John Burdon's analysis should not be taken literally. To assume that the Hausa kings gave judgments arbitrarily may imply that the judges never applied Islamic law, or that they did it to please the kings. What can be said is that they followed their customary laws, which might or might not appeal to observers or outsiders. Perhaps the Muslims who surrounded the kings and acted on their will were to blame for their silence on injustice.

Hiskett's sociological approach to relations between the Muslim elites and the Hausa kings in that period is worth noting. He contends that "two systems were struggling for supremacy on the Hausa scene: one was Islamic and the other polytheist."[68] The Muslims who attempted to conduct their lives according to Islamic principles were seen as strangers who wanted to seize power illegitimately. The polytheists, regardless of their status in the government, were too strong to be opposed by the minority Muslims. Thus the Muslims compromised by admitting their position. In Hiskett's view, the Muslims considered this type of Islam to be a political necessity. He says:

> It was a matter of balancing two sets of interests against one another, a seesaw process of constant checks and balances rather than of a slow but powerful force, moving majestically towards an inevitable climax.[69]

During the medieval stage, Islamic law was partially established as a legal institution by a visiting jurist, Muhammad 'Abd al-Kareem Ibn Muhammad al-Maghili. He resided in Katsina and established himself as a teacher and a jurist. He taught people about Islam and its laws; he consequently appointed one of his students, Muhammad ibn Muhammad al-Tazakhti, to be the first recognized judge (*qadi*).[70] He also appointed a judge in Kano and wrote a code of procedure on both civil and criminal matters to be followed by the judges. He established two courts known as the alkali[71] court and the emir court. At the alkali court, judges were assisted by scribes who were knowledgeable in Islamic law. This court had jurisdiction in civil and criminal cases, except for homicide. The second court was the emir court, with members who included the emirs themselves and some counsels.

The third stage was the stage of real implementation of Islamic law (1808–1900). That period started with the emergence of Shaykh Uthman Dan Fodio as an Islamic reformer. He charged the Habe and Hausa leaders for their failure to apply Islamic law in their private and public affairs. He waged a religious war against them and was victorious. After the *Jihad*, he established Islamic law, which his followers adhered to. He reformed the existing courts, while his son Muhammad Bello built new courts and supplied them with scholars who were knowledgeable in Islamic jurisprudence. There were three types of court at that time: the alkali court, the emir court and the appeal court. The latter was headed by the caliph.[72] The procedures and duties of these courts were explained in the works of Shaykh Uthman, Muhammad Bello and Shaykh Abdullah ibn Fodio. The functions and the procedures followed in them will be discussed in chapter 4.

Islamic Law During the British Occupation

Little can be said about this period because Islam, as a legal system, suffered much deprivation., its powers and jurisdictions being curtailed. At the same time, Islamic law underwent no development in its thought. Rather, its teaching and learning were narrow as a result of establishing English law under the canopy of legal harmony. Nevertheless, a number of changes occurred in both the so-called native and the English courts. These changes did not emanate from the Islamic perception but from the English acclaimed notion of serving the common good of the people.

Immediately after the conquest and the arrival of Lord Lugard[73] in Sokoto on March 19, 1903,[74] he appointed Muhammad Atahiru II as the leader of the Muslims and John Burdon as the resident and in charge of administration in Sokoto. Lord Lugard also declared that the British would not interfere with the religions of the natives. He followed the policy of *indirect rule* through which the emirates in the North were retained in their various positions and empowered to administer the affairs of their people. The role of the British colonial occupiers was to supervise the natives' administration and offer advice wherever needed."[75] Lugard said in his address to the people of Sokoto:

> Government will, in no way, interfere with the *Mohammedan* religion. Every person has the right to appeal to the Resident who will however endeavor to uphold the power of the native courts to deal with native cases according to the law and custom of the country.[76]

In that address he assured Northern Nigerians of British recognition and support of the local legal systems. However, in reality he could not tolerate their existence alongside the British law that he was to enforce and implement as directed by his government. In spite of his official position, he sought to change the relationship between the Islamic and British systems. He said on another occasion:

> The time is now, in my opinion, ripe for a change, but the changes must be gradually introduced if they are to be effective, and not alienate the confidence of the people.[77]

To implement the polity of change, Lugard made an announcement in which he withdrew his recognition of Islamic law and relegated it to the status of native customary laws. He curtailed the juridical power of the alkali courts and replaced them with the English courts. Moreover, the cases tried by alkali courts at the *Shari`ah* courts were subjected to passing the "repugnant test.'[78] Thus *Shari`ah* courts were placed under strict supervision of the residents, who were given unlimited power, at any stage, to assess, transfer and review any case decided by the native courts [i.e. Islamic courts].[79] All of these attempts were seen by the natives as gradual steps to whittle down Islamic and native laws and replace them with English laws. Lord Lugard announced later on in Sokoto that the fundamental law of the country should be "the common law, the doctrines of equity, and the statutes of general application, which were in force in England on January 1st 1900."[80] He believed that since those English laws were good for Britons, they must be good for Africans; he paid no attention to the native beliefs and culture.

The emirs opposed the British supervision of Islamic law. They argued that what was decided according to the *Shari`ah* should not be subject to review and reversal by an alien legal system that did not recognize the Islamic legal system. Despite their disapproval, Lugard went ahead with his policies. Thus, as evidenced above, Islamic law did not witness any development; instead it underwent curtailment and abrogation. The pretext of harmonizing both the native (Islamic law included) and English laws, as experience has shown, proved to be biased against Islamic law[81] as seen in the following two cases.

In *M. Abba v. Mary T. Baikie*, the alkali court ruled that Baikie, a Christian, could not inherit from her father [a Muslim] because of the difference in religion. The judge asserted that Islam did not allow a non-Muslim to inherit from a Muslim, nor a Muslim to inherit from a non-Muslim.[82] Baikie, dissatisfied with this judgment, appealed to the supreme court, which reversed the case on the grounds that the Islamic law provision was repugnant to natural justice and equity,[83] thus she was allowed to inherit from her father.

After this case, the Muslim judges expected that the acclaimed notion of natural justice and equity would be applied to all similar cases without discrimination and not exclusively for the assessment of Islamic law. Unfortunately the British practices proved otherwise, as in the following case.

In *Dawodu v. Danmole*,[84] the deceased left two wives, one with nine children and the other with four. According to the Yoruba law of inheritance, the deceased's property should have been distributed equally according to the number of the wives irrespective of the number of children. Thus, a mother who had ten children would share equally with a mother who had one child. In this case, one of the sons, Dawodu, appealed to the privy council for redistribution. His appeal was rejected on the grounds that the distribution was in accord with the customary law of Yoruba, and thus should be upheld. No question of compliance with natural justice and equity was raised as it was when reviewing appeals from *Shari`ah* courts.[85]

Islamic Law on the Eve of Independence in 1960

Just before Nigerian independence, Islamic law suffered another setback in its application resulting from the introduction of the Islamic penal code in Northern Nigeria in 1956. This replaced the Islamic law injunctions that were applied in criminal cases in native and emir courts. The government claimed that it introduced the penal code:

1. to bring harmony into the Nigerian legal system;
2. to remove the bad reputation that often accompanied the application of Islamic criminal law;
3. to win international support for Islamic law.[86]

However, all these claims were questionable. As stated by Bappa Mahmud,[87] later events proved that one of the objectives of the government in enforcing the Islamic Penal Code was to abolish Islamic criminal laws and to distort the minor laws retained therein as happened in its recommendation of imprisonment for adultery.[88] One would expect that when Nigeria became independent, its citizens would be free to discern the pattern of law they preferred, but reality proved otherwise.

The penal code might have been a reform based on *maslahah* (the concept of considering the interests of the public good in enacting a rule of law) had it taken into account the interests of Muslims by drawing its law from the *Shari`ah* itself. However, as seen above, it was an amalgamation of different laws with different purposes to serve different goals. It did not meet the requirements for the application of *maslahah*. Consequently, the government's attempts to reform the law were suspected of being a tool to uproot all links with Islamic law and replace it with common law.[89] This attitude was evidenced in Major Nzeogwu Chukwama's attempt to close down all native and emir courts in the north where the *Shari`ah* was being applied.[90] A few days after the Nigerian coup of 1966, he ordered that all cases in all native courts be directed to magistrates' courts. However, the order could not be implemented because there were insufficient judges at the magistrates' courts to adjudicate the cases.[91]

Another important occurrence at the advent of independence was the establishment of the *Shari`ah* Court of Appeal. A few years earlier, some minor changes had taken place—for instance, area courts[92] were introduced to replace native courts, and the former were put under the Ministry of Justice. Thus the role given to the application of Islamic law in the area court edicts was limited.[93] Nevertheless, the objectives of the *Shari`ah* court of appeal, as announced by its promoters, were to rectify the mistakes made by the lower courts. The debate about whether to establish a Muslim court of appeal was intense. Although many supported it, there were some prominent scholars of Islamic law inside and outside Nigeria at that time who did not hesitate to express their dissatisfaction with *Shari`ah* law.[94] However, the call for the establishment of a Muslim court of appeal prevailed because of the recommendation of the Brooke Commission of Inquiry. With its establishment in 1956, Muslims were permitted to appeal to it but its jurisdiction was also narrowed. Appeals from the Muslim court of appeal go to the high court of appeal (whose members must include at least one Muslim scholar learned in Islamic law) and then to the federal court of appeal (whose members also may or may not include Muslim scholars).[95] When members of this court include a Muslim scholar, the said Muslim must have been called to the bar and served for at least twelve years in the administration of justice at the state or federal level.

The *Shari`ah* Court of Appeal's jurisdiction is confined to Muslim personal law.[96] It is not the last court; appeals from it are taken to the high court of appeal of the state or to the federal court of appeal from the high court.[97]

In 1976 the Area Courts Reform Committee recommended in its report that the *Shari`ah* Court of Appeal be allowed to hear appeals in all civil matters emanating from area courts.[98] Muslim judges argued that the cases going to high courts from the *Shari`ah* court of appeal were being decided by incompetent judges in Islamic law. And because the high court ruled in 1982 that Muslims should have no right to be judges at the high court to hear appeals on Islamic law, the *qadis* (Muslim judges) were excluded from sitting as members on the grounds that Section 238 of the 1979 Constitution did not provide for that as Section 53 of the 1963 Constitution had done.[99]

Decree 26 of 1986 gives the *Shari`ah* Court of Appeal the jurisdiction in all Islamic civil matters decided in the court of first instance that has been provided for in Section 256 of the draft of the reviewed constitution.[100] In general, then, Islamic law in Nigerian Constitution of 1979 may be seen thus:

1. Islamic law is a recognized law and one of the three systems of law operating in Nigeria. The other systems are English law and native law.
2. Its application is confined to personal law of marriage, divorce, preemption (*waqf*) gift, will, child custody and any other question to which the parties consent (Sec. 184 of the draft constitution).
3. The Islamic courts are to enforce and apply Maliki law only, and this law is also subject to customary interpretation in Nigeria (Sec. 189 [5]).

Conclusion

It is worth noting that the government of the Federal Republic of Nigeria, as well as some judges at the high courts and federal courts of appeal, expressed their uneasiness about the application of Islamic law. They feared that the *Shari`ah* would become a rival to common law. They attempted to whittle down Islamic law, but in spite of their efforts the practice of the *Shari`ah* in the northern states persists. In his last years as governor general for Nigeria, Lord Lugard's attempts to reduce the Islamic courts failed because he did not have competent people to administer justice in the Hausa land. The efforts of Major Nzeogwu Chukwama to uproot all native courts did not succeed either because the dispensation of justice in the magistrates' courts is expensive and corrupt. Nevertheless, the native courts (Islamic courts included) had the privilege of adjudicating nearly 90% of all civil cases (in 1967) in the north.[101]

It is observable from the position of Islamic law from 1900 until 1980 that there was a lack of development of thought in the *Shari`ah*; no provocative issues were raised, and no new ideas were generated for discourse. Nearly all of the public arguments about the application of

Islamic law in Nigeria were concerned with the procedure to be followed in administering justice. Many Nigerians do not know what system of law has been applied to them, and those who do hardly care about where the law comes from as long as they are not involved or directly affected by it.[102]

It could be asserted that responsibility for the lack of development of thought in Islamic law in Nigeria rests with the inclination of Muslim scholars at that time to safeguard the influence left to them by the government. They believed that there was little, if any, advantage in generating new ideas if there was no chance for their application. Thus they preferred to protect the family law niche where Islamic law was permitted to function. It is apparent that whenever the government is bent on reducing the application of Islamic law, Muslims become more attached to the letter of the law. This attitude often leads some Muslim scholars to protect a practice that may not be a recommended practice but that is a custom of a particular group or tribe which has been clothed in an Islamic "robe."

The subjection of Islamic law to the test of repugnancy (i.e. that Islamic law should not be repugnant to natural justice, equity or good conscience) unfortunately puts the *Shari`ah* on a low level, while common law has been given public recognition by force.

Notes

1. It should be pointed out that Islam reached Africa prior to arriving in many Arab countries. Islam was in Ethiopia before it was introduced to Medina, Egypt, Iraq, Syria and all other Arab countries, so it is not new to Africans. The first migration of the followers of Muhammad from Mecca was to Abyssinia, and among those who went was the daughter of Muhammad, Ruqayyah bint Muhammad. She was accompanied by her husband Uthman bin Affan, who later became the third caliph after the death of Muhammad.
2. W. R. Crocker, *Nigeria: A Critique of British Colonial Administration* (London: George Allen & Unwin Ltd., 1936), p. 213.
3. Crocker, p. 213.
4. Sulayman S. Nyang, *Islam, Christianity and African Identity* (Vermont: Amana Books, 1984), pp. 66–67.
5. A Rashid Motin, "Political Dynamism of Islam in Nigeria," *Islamic Studies* 26, no. 2 (1987): 180. See also Peter Clarke, *West Africa and Islam* (London: Edward Arnold Ltd., 1982), pp. 66–67.
6. Mervyn Hiskett, *The Development of Islam in West Africa* (London: Longman, 1984), p. 59.

7. Hiskett, p. 63.
8. Hiskett, p. 63.
9. Hiskett, p. 66.
10. S.J. Hogben, *An Introduction to the History of Islamic States of Northern Nigeria* (Ibadan: Oxford University Press, 1967), p. 50.
11. Hogben does not mention by name the rulers who embraced Islam and later went back to their native religion. However, the possibility of such conversion to the native religions cannot be denied.
12. Mai is a title for the post of king in the Bornu Empire.
13. Louis Brenner, "Muhammad Amin al-Kanam and Religion and Politics in Bornu," in *Studies in West African Islamic History*, ed. John Ralph Willis (Totowa, N.J: Frank Cass, 1979), vol. 1, p. 161.
14. Peter B. Clarke, *West Africa and Islam* (London: Edward Arnold Ltd., 1982), p. 71.
15. Clarke, p. 68.
16. A. A. Gwandu, "Aspects of the Administration of Justice in the Sokoto Caliphate and Shaykh Abdullah Ibn Fodio's Contribution to it," in *Islamic Law in Nigeria: Application & Teaching*, ed. S. K. Rashid (Lagos: Islamic Publication Bureau, 1986), p. 11; Clarke, p. 66.
17. Hausa land is what is known today as the Northern Nigeria, especially Sokoto, Kano, Katsina, Bornu and Niger states.
18. Motin, p. 180; Hogben, p. 17; Clarke, p. 60.
19. Clarke, p. 60.
20. Clarke, p. 60.
21. Clarke, p. 62.
22. Clarke, p. 62.
23. Clarke, p. 62.
24. Musa Ali Ajetummobi, "Shari`ah Legal Practice in Nigeria: 1956–83" (PhD diss.) University of Ilorin, Department of Islamic Studies, June 1988), pp. 39–40.
25. Gwandu, pp. 11–12.
26. The Habe were the Hausa people who were neither a separate tribe nor race. They were groups of scattered people from different origins. They lived in the city-states mostly in northwest Nigeria and spoke Hausa. See Hogben, pp. 76–77.
27. Gwandu, pp. 11–12.
28. Gwandu, pp. 13–14; see also Clarke, p. 113.
29. Gwandu, p. 12.
30. Gwandu, p. 12.
31. Miton, p. 180.
32. Ibraheem Sulaiman, *The Islamic State and the Challenge of History* (New York: Mansell Publishing Ltd., 1987), pp. 4–5; see also Hogben, p. 55.

33. The *Jihad* of Uthman in Hausa land has generated a lot of controversy regarding whether it was a religious or a racial war between the Fulanis and the Hausas. For full elaboration of that assessment, see M. G. Smith, "The Jihad of Shehu Dan Fodio: Some Problem," *Islam in Tropical Africa*, ed. I. M. Lewis (Bloomington: Indiana University Press, 1964), pp. 213–225.
34. Clarke, pp. 117–118.
35. By 1806 there were about twenty-five judges appointed by Shaykh Uthman. All were administering justice according to Islamic law in the Sokoto Caliphate. See Ahmad Beita Yusuf, "Legal Pluralism in the Northern States of Nigeria: Conflict of Laws in a Multi-Ethnic Environment" (unpublished PhD diss., State University of New York, Buffalo, 1976), p. 46.
36. Murray Last, *The Sokoto Caliphate* (New York: Humanities Press, 1967), p. 49.
37. Among the many judges he appointed were Muhammad Sambo, the chief judge of Sokoto; Abu Bakar Ladan Rame, a judge for Sifawa; Shaykh Bilali and Muhammad ibn Muhammad Binduwo. See Last, pp. 49–50.
38. Hasan Gwarzo, "The Development of the Implementation of *Shari`ah* in Northern States" (paper presented at a seminar organized by the Department of Islamic Studies in cooperation with the Department of Arabic and Faculty of Law, Bayero University, Kano,March 23, 1985), p. 6.
39. Sulaiman, *The Islamic State*, pp. 44–47.
40. Ibraheem Sulaiman, *A Revolution in History: The Jihad of Uthman Dan Fodio* (New York: Mansell Publishing Ltd., 1986), pp. 156–60.
41. Sulaiman, *The Islamic State*, pp. 61–62, quoting Shehu Uthman, *Tabsirat al-Mubtadi' fi Usul al-Din*. See also Ismail Balogun, *The Life and Works of Uthman Dan Fodio* (Lagos: Islamic Publishing Bureau, 1975), pp. 50–51. It is pertinent to point out here that Shaykh Uthman Dan Fodio followed the Maliki school of law. He occasionally accepted other opinions from other schools.
42. Balogun, p. 51.
43. Sulaiman, *A Revolution*, p. 157.
44. Sulaiman, *A Revolution*, p. 157.
45. See Uthman Dan Fodio's work *Irshad al-Ummah ila Taysir al-Millah* , M.S., N.H.R.S. 8/1 Zaria, p. 7; see also A. M. Hajj Nour, "An Elementary Study in the *Fiqh* of Dan Fodio," in *Studies in the History of the Sokoto Caliphate: The Sokoto Seminar Papers* (Lagos: Third Press International, 1979), pp. 225–226.
46. Sulaiman, *A Revolution*, p. 156; see also Hajj Nour, p. 224.
47. Sulaiman, *A Revolution*, p. 156.
48. Sulaiman, *A Revolution*, p. 159.
49. Ibraheem Sulaiman is a senior lecturer in law in the Faculty of Law at Ahmadu Bello University, Nigeria. He is a leading writer on the history of

jihad of Shaykh Uthman Dan Fodio and is also recognized by some Nigerians as an Islamic activist. For more information about him, see Allan Christelow, "Three Islamic Voices in Contemporary Nigeria", in *Islam and Political Economy of Meaning: Comparative Studies of Muslim Discourse*, ed. by William R. Roff, (London: Croom Helm, 1987), pp. 237–244.

50. The property here includes houses, and Muslim men and women who were captured during the war by non-Muslims and put into slavery. Of course, there was no exchange of prisoners of war at that time.
51. Sulaiman, *A Revolution*, pp. 159–160.
52. Sulaiman, *A Revolution*, p. 160.
53. During the Shaykh Uthman's life, however, Islamic law was applied in the whole of the Sokoto Caliphate. Literature on how justice should be administered and applied was produced by Shaykh Uthman, who, during the last years of his life, withdrew from the political scene and activities, devoting his time instead to scholarly works.
54. An example of adherence to the letter of the law was the case of Sultan Muhammad Attahiru I (1901–1902), who left his empire in Sokoto to be conquered by Lord Lugard and his army. Sultan Attahiru interpreted the law such that if non-believers were to come while the Muslims were weak militarily, the Muslims should undertake a migration [*hijrah*] because it is unlawful for non-believers to dominate Muslims. He forgot that Shaykh Uthman, Muhammad Bello and Abdullah fought for the establishment of the Islamic state and they did not run away from the non-believers. Unfortunately for Sultan Attahiru I, he was killed at Burmi by Lugard's army. See Smith, pp. 236–47.
55. These books include *Ihya al-Sunnah wa Ikhmad al-Bid'a*, *Tawqif al-Muslimin'ala Hukm Madhhab al-Mujtahidin* and *Irshad al-Ummah*, all written by Shaykh Uthman Dan Fodio; and *Diya al-Hukkam* by Abdullah ibn Fodio. They were written as guides for the judges to assist them in dispensing their duties. See Ajetunmobi, pp. 45–46.
56. Clarke, p. 115.
57. Alan C. Burns, *History of Nigeria* (London: George Allen & Unwin Ltd., 1948), p. 48.
58. A similar tax still prevails in some major cities of Northern Nigeria, such as Kano and Zaria. In both of these cities, everyone who enters the local motor park must pay a tax of four kobo whether they are traveling or not. The driver of the taxi or truck they board must pay a tax for picking up passengers from the park, and also another tax of fifty kobo or one naira at the gate before they are allowed to leave the park. This practice is totally unIslamic and unfair because no service whatsoever is rendered to escort visitors to the motor park. It is very unfortunate that every government in both Kano and Kaduna states approves these unfair taxes and no attempt

is made to eradicate them. The most painful thing about this is that the people ascribe such taxes to Islam and claim that the Sokoto Caliphate endorsed them.

59. Succession to the throne and official posts became hereditary in the Sokoto Caliphate without any consideration of the consequences. Posts of the fathers are automatically inherited by their sons or by close relatives. Last cites a few examples of this in *The Sokoto Caliphate*, p. 84.
60. That the appointment of imamship should be based on merit is controversial in Islamic political thought because there are a number of interpretations as to how Muslim leaders were appointed or selected after the Prophet Muhammad. However, there is a saying of the Prophet which states that the imams should be from the Quraysh tribe. It was on that basis that Abu Bakr, 'Umar and 'Uthman were selected. But this view did not appeal to the Kharijite sect, which claims that imamship should be based on merit. This latter view is gaining greater acceptance among Muslims today.
61. It is interesting to note that the method of appointing or electing imamship was discussed by both Shaykh Uthman and Abdullah in their works. Uthman stated in *Najmu al-Ikhwan* that hereditary kingship was illegal in Islamic law, although the son or relative of the deceased imam could be appointed if he possessed the requisite qualifications for leadership. On the other hand, Shehu Abdullah insisted that appointment by inheritance was against Islamic law and should be avoided by all means if the state was to be run on the basis of the *Sunnah* of the Prophet Muhammad. Abdullah cited the cases of the Prophet, Abu Bakr and 'Umar, and asserted that all were succeeded not by their sons or close relatives but by those deemed eligible and selected by the electoral committee. See Sulaiman, *A Revolution*, pp. 152–53, 96–97. Despite this argument, Shaykh Uthman appointed his son, and by doing so he set a precedent that was responsible for one of the causes of decadence in the Sokoto Caliphate.
62. For more information on this subject, see *A Revolution*, p. 166, fn 8.
63. For more information about Shaykh Uthman's scholarship, see Balogun's *The Life and Works of Shehu Uthman Dan Fodio*. Balogun mentions the names of the books that Uthman wrote, he gives the titles of those which had been published and translated into English, and he states where to find the manuscripts.
64. [91] Yusuf Bala Usman, "The Transformation of Political Communities: Some Notes on the Perception of a Significant Dimension of the Sokoto Jihad," in *Studies in the History of The Sokoto Caliphate*, pp. 34–55. The author surveys the different perspectives of many writers and how they perceived the Sokoto *Jihad*. He inclines to the notion that the Sokoto *Jihad* was a racial war between the rich Hausas and the poor Fulanis.
65. Gwarzo, pp. 3–6.
66. Gwarzo, pp. 5–6.

67. J. A. Burdon, *Northern Nigeria: Historical Notes on Certain Emirates and Tribes* (London: Farnborough, Gregg, 1972), p. 94 (reprint).
68. Hiskett, p. 80.
69. Hiskett, p. 80.
70. Gwarzo, p. 3.
71. An alkali court is a lower court headed by a judge who is learned in Islamic law. Usually the judge decides the cases by himself. An emir court is composed of the emir of the city and a number of persons who are learned in Islamic law as assessors.
72. Last, p. 49.
73. Lord Lugard was governor of the northern states of Nigeria at that time. For his policies regarding Northern Nigeria, see A. H. M. Greene, *Lugard and the Amalgamation of Nigeria: A Documentary Record*, London: Frank Cass & Co. Ltd., 1968.
74. Hoghen, p. 215.
75. Crocker, p. 213.
76. Lord Fredrick Lugard, *Political Memoranda* (London: Frank Cass & Co. Ltd., 1970), p. 272.
77. Lugard, p. 272.
78. Lugard, p. 84. The repugnant test means that Islamic law should not be repugnant to natural justice, equity and good conscience. Using this test, a restriction was put on the operation of Islamic law covering what the colonial British considered to be inhumane punishment, such as mutilation of a thief's hand or killing a person who had committed homicide. See Hiskett, p. 277.
79. Abdul Malik Bappa Mahmud, *A Brief History of Shari`ah in the Defunct Northern Nigeria* (Jos: Jos University Press, 1988), pp. 9–11. See also Lugard's Political Memoranda, pp. 90–91, par. 17; J. N. D Anderson, *Islamic Law in Africa* (London: Colonial Research Publication, 1954), p. 175.
80. Lugard, p. 83.
81. Ajetunmobi, pp. 67–68.
82. Case no. K/20A/1943.
83. Bappa Mahmud, p. 16. The judges in this court failed to recognize that allowing sons or daughters to inherit from their parents is a conventional law rather than a natural right. The parents have a choice to exclude their descendants from inheriting from them if they wish.
84. 1962 (1. W.L.R.) 1053.
85. For more information about similar cases, see A. O. Obilade, *The Nigerian Legal System* (London: Sweet & Maxwell, 1979), pp. 86–87.
86. Ajetunmobi, pp. 72–74. What astonished a researcher was the committee's big assertion in its concluding part of the white paper of the report that

"the government is satisfied that there is nothing repugnant to Islam in these reforms but that, on the contrary, their introduction without delay is essential if the region (North) is to avoid internal disputes, live in harmony with the rest of the Federation and gain international acceptance after independence for its judicial and legal system." See Ajetunmobi, p. 74, quoting from *Statement by the Government of the Northern Region of Nigeria on the Re-Organization of the Legal and Judicial Systems of the Northern Region* (*SGNRNRLJSNR*), Kaduna, Government Printer, 1958, para. 36.

87. Bappa Mahmud is the grand kadi (chief judge of the *Shari`ah* court of appeal) of Bauchi State in Nigeria. He is considered by Nigerian lawyers as a liberal scholar in terms of the application of Islamic law. He often emphasizes the notion of justice and fair play in his writings and discourse. For more information about his ideas about justice, see Christelow, pp. 237–244.
88. Bappa Mahmud, pp. 25–26.
89. Ajetunmobi, pp. 82–83; Mahmud, pp. 30–31.
90. Mahmud, p. 30.
91. Mahmud, pp. 30–31.
92. Area court is the new name given to the former native court. Native court was the name given by the British colonials to the alkali court after the conquest of Sokoto in 1903. The word "native" was used then to neutralize the existing courts, which were Islamic, from their religious connotations.
93. Ajetunmobi, pp. 84–85.
94. Ajetunmobi, pp. 90–91; Mahmud, p. 35.
95. Ajetunmobi, pp. 94–95.
96. Ajetunmobi, p. 91.
97. Ajetunmobi, p. 92.
98. Muhammad Bashir Sambo, "Shari`ah in a Multi-Religious State: Its Application and Limitations." (paper presented at the Association of Nigerian Legal Practitioners, Lagos, February 1986), p. 11.
99. Sambo, p. 12.
100. Sambo, p. 13.
101. Mahmud, p. 31. The author mentioned that in 1964 alone, the native courts (the *Shari`ah* courts and area courts) handled 223,262 cases, while the English courts and Magistrates' courts handled only 1961 cases.
102. Generally, Nigerians hate to go to court—it is the last place to go to resolve conflicts. "No more friendly relationship after the court decision," many Nigerians believe.

CHAPTER 3

Islamic Law (the *Shari`ah*) After Independence

Introduction

From military regimes 1966 until 1979, and from 1984 until May 1999, Nigeria was ruled by successive military regimes. In 1999 a new civilian president, Olusegun Obasanjo, was elected. He vowed to bring the country back to democracy. He adopted a new constitution, which recognizes three legal systems: English common law, customary law and Islamic law. From 1903, these systems were in operation except that native law was not charged with adjudicating criminal, homicide or murder cases.

Indeed, the debate about the application of Islamic law resurfaced in Nigeria when the late General Muritala Muhammad appointed Constitution Drafting Committee (CDC) of fifty to write a new constitution as part of the move toward a return to civilian government. Headed by Chief Rotimi Williams, the CDC submitted a draft constitution to the federal military government. A year later the former chief of staff, Major General Shehu Musa Yar Adu'a gave Nigerians the chance to debate publicly the contents of the draft before it was passed into law. One of the topics that drew ambivalent attention from the public was the CDC's recommendation for the establishment of a *Shari`ah* Court of Appeal in states where the *Shari`ah* system was in operation. The committee also recommended the establishment of a federal *Shari`ah* court of appeal to hear appeal cases from the state levels.[1]

According to Salahu-deen Yusuf,[2] the CDC called for the establishment of a *Shari`ah* Court of Appeal and a federal *Shari`ah* court only in those

Y. Sodiq, *A History of the Application of Islamic Law in Nigeria*,
DOI 10.1007/978-3-319-50600-5_3

states that were already applying Islamic law. He pointed out that the committee did not recommend extending the jurisdiction of the existing aspects of the Islamic personal law in terms of its content or over whom it should apply in Nigeria,[3] as confirmed by Chief Rotimi Williams, who chaired the committee:

> The C.D.C has not made any provision in the Constitution to the effect that Islamic law should be enforced in any state in this Federation ... What the Draft Constitution has done is to give recognition to the existence of the present system by making provision for the establishment of a Shari`ah Court of Appeal in those states of the Federation where it operates at present[4]

Surprisingly, both Christians and Muslims took the recommendation of the CDC out of context. Each group gave its own interpretation but implied that the committee recommended the extension of Islamic law to areas where it had not been in operation, and that Islamic law should be the law of Nigeria. Dr Sam Babs Mala (an Islamist at the University of Jos) also misread the CDC's recommendation:

> This tendency was best seen in Nigeria at about 1977–78 during the *Shari'a* debate, centering on whether or not constitutional provision should be made for the establishment of a federal *Shari'a* court of Appeal and for *Shari'a* courts at the state level where they did not already exist.[5]

Joseph Kenny[6] assumed that the CDC's recommendation for the establishment of a federal *Shari`ah* Court of Appeal was "one further step in a plan to turn the country into an Islamic State."[7] Kenny did not stop at misreading the content of the committee's recommendation. He added in his article "Christian–Muslim Relations in Nigeria" that the former British colonial officer, Martin Dent, who argued in favor of the *Shari`ah* in Nigeria, should be considered either ignorant or a hypocrite, for how could such a person (who was supposed to promote Christianity) support the application of Islamic law?[8]

Also, Peter Clarke gave the impression that the CDC recommended the establishment of a *Shari`ah* Court of Appeal where it did not exist.[9] Both Kenny and Clarke deliberately added the phrase "where it did not exist" to the original content. By so doing, they changed the whole meaning and implication of the report.

What Is at Stake Regarding the Application of the *Shari`ah*?

There are several issues. Some are religious, some are political and some are moral. Major areas of controversy are questions about the constitutionality of the *Shari`ah*:

1. Is the application of the *Shari`ah* constitutional?
2. Is the application of the Shari`ah discriminatory?
3. Does the application of the Shari`ah violate the principle of separation between the state and the religion?
4. Is Nigeria a secular or a religious state?
5. Does the application of the Shari`ah promote justice and fairness for all Nigerians as the advocates of the Shari`ah proclaim?

Arguments for the Application of the *Shari`ah*

The proponents of the *Shari`ah* argue as follows:

1. The 1999 Constitution guarantees freedom of religion to all of Nigeria's citizens. Nigerian Muslims are Nigerians, thus they are entitled to freedom of religion. And since the application of the *Shari`ah* and abiding by *Shari`ah* law is central to the practicing of Islamic religion, Muslims should be free to adhere to their religion. Any denial of the *Shari`ah* is tantamount to the denial of religious freedom for Muslims. Their right to religious practice/freedom is expressed in Section 38 (1) of the Constitution:

> Every person shall be entitled to freedom of thought, conscience and religion, including freedom to change his religion or belief, and freedom (either alone or in community with others, and in public or private) to manifest and propagate his religion or belief in worship, teaching, practice and observance.[10]

Muslims claim that they would not have any degree of authenticity—that is, not be truly practical Muslims—if they weren't governed by the *Shari`ah*.[11] It is argued, therefore that Nigerian Muslims, wherever they live or dwell, whether as minority or majority, claim to have a moral and a legal duty to adhere to their religion and to the *Shari`ah,* unless they are denied the freedom to do so. They opt for Islamic law as a result of their conviction in its ultimate goals of substantive justice and betterment of their social and moral lives.[12]

Those who oppose the *Shari`ah* argue that recognizing Islam as a religion, and the freedom to be a Muslim, does not imply the demand to be governed by Islamic law. If that assumption was accepted, every adherent of any religion in Nigeria would be allowed to apply their religious laws, and that would be tantamount to having several legal systems. Such an allowance would not maintain Nigeria as a unified country.

2. The 1999 Constitution provides for the establishment of three legal systems: common law, customary law and the *Shari`ah.* Separate courts are established for each legal system: "There shall be a *Shari`ah* Court of Appeal of the Federal Capital Territory, Abuja" (Section 260 (1). Thus when the Constitution permits the establishment of *Shari`ah* courts and *Shari`ah* courts of appeal, it recognizes and acknowledges as legitimate a set of laws based on the Islamic faith and its tenets. Therefore the application of the *Shari`ah* is constitutional. Each state is allowed to establish a *Shari`ah* court and it is empowered to adjudicate all Islamic personal laws as well as any other jurisdiction which the National Assembly or state assembly (of any state) confers on it, as stated in section 262 (1) and 277 (1) of the 1999 Constitution. The *Shari`ah* Court of Appeal shall, in addition to such other jurisdiction as may be conferred on it by an act of the National Assembly, exercise such appellate and supervisory jurisdiction in civil proceedings involving questions of Islamic personal law (Section 262 (1).

In response to this argument, the opponents of the *Shari`ah* argue that the problem is not the establishment of a *Shari`ah* court in itself but the expansion of its jurisdiction to cover all aspects of life, especially criminal cases, which will make the *Shari`ah* a rival, and superior, to common law.

3. The proponents of the *Shari`ah* also argue that since the Constitution permits the application of *the Shari`ah,* it must be implemented fully because *the Shari`ah* is an organic whole which allows no partial application. Its partial application would amount to the invalidity of the whole Islamic legal system. Thus, to avoid this partial implementation,

the *Shari`ah court* should be given the power to adjudicate all Islamic laws whether they are criminal, civil or business law, as conferred to it by the State House of Assembly. The *Shari`ah* can function smoothly and demonstrate its efficacy when it is applied fully.[13]

4. In addition, the proponents also argue that *the Shari`ah* would only be applied on Muslims in the north. Since the majority of people in Northern Nigeria are Muslim, it was considered to be within the premise of justice and fairness that the law, which commands the approval of the majority, has the right to become the law of the State. On the other hand, the non-Muslim minority have the right to take their case to common law or customary courts, which are established in each state of the federation.[14] Non-Muslims are not forced to adjudicate via *the Shari`ah*. Perhaps, if they opt for it, they would not be denied it. However, it would be unfair for Muslims who are in the majority (in the north) to be asked by the minority to abandon their rights and to practice laws that are against their convictions.

In response to this argument, the opponents of *the Shari`ah* reject the unsupported claim that Muslims are in the majority in Northern Nigeria. They argue that this claim has no empirical evidence.[15] On the other hand, they say that the majority have not been asked whether they want *the Shari`ah* to be applied to them. The opponents claim that it was a few people, especially those in authority who want to impose *the Shari`ah* on their subjects (the general public in the states that apply *the Shari`ah*) who began to petition the chief justice of the federation, Godwin Agabi, to stop the application of *the Shari`ah*. Thus on March 18, 2002, Agabi issued a statement and declared the application of *the Shari`ah* to be unconstitutional and discriminatory, and he appealed to all states to stop doing so.[16]

5. The proponents of the *Shari`ah* further argue that Nigeria before and after independence has had multijudicial systems: common law, the *Shari`ah* and customary law. If the Muslims decide to expand the *Shari`ah* to include criminal cases, a matter which affects them, they should be free to do so. They question why other religious groups should not recognize the expansion of the *Shari`ah*, while common law is expanded and modified at any time and no one raises any objection.

Arguments Against the Application of *Shari`ah*

Many people who oppose the application of the *Shari`ah* in Nigeria have little knowledge of Nigerian law, which recognizes three legal systems. They are unaware that the *Shari`ah* was in full operation before the arrival of the colonial regime and that it has never disappeared. Of course, its application has always been a cause of tension among political leaders. At times, some areas of *Shari`ah* jurisdiction are curtailed and at others they are retained. Even in the south, among the Yorubas, the demand for the application of *the Shari`ah* was been recorded as early as the 1890s.[17] Kwara State, whose citizens are Yorubas, has applied the *Shari`ah* since independence and has a *Shari`ah* Court of Appeal.

1. The first argument of the opponents of *the Shari`ah* is that Nigeria is a secular country. It prohibits the adoption of any state religion as espoused in Section 10 of the 1999 Constitution: "The Government of the Federation or of a State shall not adopt any religion as State religion." The establishment of Islamic courts and implementation of the *Shari`ah* by several states in the north are considered and interpreted as an adoption of Islam as the religion of the state. In other words, allowing the *Shari`ah* to be implemented negates the "noble" concept of the separation of state and religion. The government should maintain its secular status by not approving any religion to be the religion of any state in Nigeria. Also, taxpayers' money should not be spent on establishing Islamic courts, which directly or indirectly promote Islam over other religions.

The proponents of *the Shari`ah* respond to this argument by stating that the endorsement of *the Shari`ah* as a legal system of a state does not constitute the adoption of Islam as a state religion, which is prohibited in Section 10 of the Constitution. The former chief justice of Nigeria, Justice Mohammed Bello, points out that the Constitution stops short of whether a state can adopt established religious laws or enact laws based on religion. He argues that those twelve states which decided to apply the *Shari`ah* have not adopted or declared Islam as a state religion. They have adopted *the Shari`ah* as the governing law in their states just as the southern states have adopted common or customary laws. The adoption of a particular legal system does not violate the rule of separation between state and religion, or the Constitution, in any sense. "The *Shari`ah*,"

Bello adds, "through the deliberate constitutionally permissible establishment of the *Shari`ah* courts and *Shari`ah* courts of appeal, is intended to run concurrently with any other laws [in Nigeria]."[18] Hence the fact that Nigeria is a secular state does not mean that its citizens cannot choose the *Shari`ah* as their governing law. They are free to do so.

Further, a secular state should not be conceived as an anti-religious state. It is a state which cares about the interests of its citizens regardless of their beliefs. It must treat all of its population fairly, promoting their rights and protecting their religious freedom. If non-Muslims opt for a law that suits their religion, they should be entitled to it just as Muslims are. However, they should not enforce their religions on others, just as *Shari`ah* advocates should not enforce *the Shari`ah* on non-Muslims.

Therefore the argument that the application of *the Shari`ah* is unconstitutional because it violates the principle of separation of the state from religion is weak. The 1999 Constitution endorses the establishment of different legal systems and, since the *Shari`ah* court is permitted to be established, the government knows for sure that *the Shari`ah* court will apply Islamic laws. Sections 260 and 275 of the Constitution give recognition and acknowledgement to *the Shari`ah:* "There shall be for any State that requires it a Shari`ah Court of Appeal for that State" (Section 275).

In each state that applies the *Shari`ah* there are area courts,[19] which adjudicate Islamic personal laws. Appeals from area courts go to the *Shari`ah* Court of Appeal in the state, appeals from the *Shari`ah* courts of appeal go to the state high court, and appeals from the state high court go to the supreme/federal court of Nigeria in Kaduna or Lagos, which has the finality of determinations as expressed in Section 235 of the 1999 Constitution.

2. The second argument by the opponents of the *Shari`ah* is that the application of the *Shari`ah* in full scale and to all aspects of Muslim life will amount to its supremacy over the Constitution. While the Constitution is supreme according to Section 1, the *Shari`ah*, unfortunately in theory, does not permit or admit the supremacy of any other laws as pointed out by Justice Bello. In this sense the *Shari`ah* is a rival to the Constitution. However, in application, anyone who does not agree with the decision of the *Shari`ah* court can appeal to a higher court or to the supreme high court, which maintains the final decision. Thus, in practice, the Constitution is supreme; the *Shari`ah* is inferior and the decisions of the *Shari`ah* courts,

including the state *Shari`ah* Court of Appeal, are subject to change and modification, or even nullification, by the supreme high court. There are a few appeal cases which went from the *Shari`ah* courts to the supreme court, where the latter reversed the decision of the *Shari`ah* Court of Appeal, such as *Karimatu Yakubu and Alhaji Mahmud Ndatsu v. Alhaji Yakubu Tafida Paiko and Alhaji Umaru Gwagwada.*[20]

3. Another strong argument against the *Shari`ah* has a political overtone. It states that a full application of the *Shari`ah* is politically motivated to weaken the government of the elected president, Olusegun Obasanjo, who is a Christian from the south. And instead of paying attention to the needs of the state, the authorities pay great attention to religious matters at the expense of these needs, thus distracting the public from the important things to less important issues. The opponents stressed that the Muslims from the north were in the position of leadership from 1979 to 1999, yet they failed to implement the *Shari`ah* on a full scale. Why is it that during Obasanjo's presidency they wanted total implementation of the *Shari`ah* if not for political purposes and to create tension among the political parties?

Nobody doubts the political motivation of the *Shari`ah*, but Islam does not differentiate between religion and politics. Other political parties utilize politics to advance their interests and fulfill their goals, whether those goals or objectives are religious or not. Political parties often seize an opportune time to advance their own interests and promote their own agenda. President Obasanjo acknowledged the political motivation of the *Shari`ah*. When he was asked to react against the application of the *Shari`ah*, he refrained and responded that the *Shari`ah* as projected by the northerners was a political game and it would soon fade away.[21]

4. The opponents also argue that the *Shari`ah* has been used to oppress those in poverty. They cite a few cases where poor people were convicted of crimes and punished, while the elite and the rich who committed similar crimes were not persecuted to the same degree. For instance, when Peri Partum Bariya was convicted of fornication, she received eighty lashes and the man who fornicated with her was set free for lack of adequate evidence and witnesses to convict him. In addition, the hands of those who stole cows, donkeys, goats and a few naira were severed, while the government workers and officers

who embezzled millions of naira were not convicted and punished merely because they were sufficiently wealthy to hire lawyers to take their cases to trial and plead for them.[22]

5. Further, the opponents argue that the *Shari`ah* is imposed on non-Muslims despite the promise that it will not be applied to them. Mbahi in his article "Shari`ah, Northern Ethnic and Religious Minority and the Federal Government: A Perspective" cites the pronouncement of the governor of Yobe State, who declared that he would start compelling non-Muslim women to cover their heads (wear a *hijab*). Mbahi wonders how an elected governor, who is presumably charged with the protection of the overall interests of all members of his state, regardless of their religious beliefs, could attempt to enforce this practice.[23]

It is this sort of approach and the attempt from the higher authorities in the state to impose Islamic laws on non-Muslims that the masses object to. In my view, this is a misuse of power by the governor of Yobe. The Constitution does not grant any power to a governor, or anyone else, to tell people what to wear or how to dress. Islam only encourages Muslims (males and females) to dress modestly. Muslim leaders should not impose any dress code on anyone. If they do, they should be challenged and brought to justice.

6. One of the strongest arguments against the *Shari`ah* lies in the claim that its application is discriminatory in the sense that Muslims receive harsher punishment than any other Nigerians who commit the same crime. And since the Constitution prohibits such discrimination, it follows that the application of the *Shari`ah*, especially the criminal laws, is unconstitutional, as stated below.

A citizen of Nigeria of a particular community, ethnic group, place of origin, sex, religion or political opinion shall not, by reason only that he is such a person,

> be subjected either expressly by, or in the practical application of, any law in force in Nigeria or any executive or administrative action of the government, to disabilities or restrictions to which citizens of Nigeria of other communities, ethnic groups, places of origin, sex, religions or political opinions are not made subject. (Section 42) (1A)

Based on this section, the chief justice of the federation, Godwin Agabi, wrote a letter to the twelve states that apply the *Shari`ah*, stating that they should stop administering Islamic law because its application is inconsistent with the Constitution and because it is discriminatory against the Muslims. He requested that both individuals and states should comply with the provision of the Constitution. In his letter he said:

> The fact that *Shari`ah* law applies only to Moslems or to those who elect to be bound by it makes imperative that the rights of such persons to equality with other citizens under the Constitution be not infringed. A Moslem should not be subjected to a punishment more severe than would be imposed on other Nigerians for the same offence. Equality before the law means that Moslems should not be discriminated against. As an elected Governor, I am certain that you would not tolerate such disparity in the allocation of punishment. It is not only against the Constitution but also against equity and good conscience. Individuals and states must comply with the Constitution. A court, which imposes discriminatory punishments, is deliberately flouting the Constitution. The stability, unity and integrity of the nation are threatened by such action. In order to implement policies or programmes inconsistent with the Constitution we must first secure its amendment. Until that is done, we have to abide by it. To proceed on the basis either that the Constitution does not exist or that it is irrelevant is to deny the existence of the nation itself. We cannot deny the rule of law and hope to have peace and stability.[24]

His letter implies that the application of the *Shari`ah* is an arbitrary implementation and amounts to the denial of the "existence of the nation itself."

Many writers consider the above argument the strongest one against the implementation of the *Shari`ah* because this analysis/refutation came from the chief justice and the attorney general of the Federal Republic of Nigeria. However, under critical examination it appears to be unconvincing in that the application of the *Shari`ah* does not amount to discrimination against Muslims. If what the chief justice meant by discrimination is to apply different rules to different individuals for the same offence, one could argue that there would be different punishments for the same offence when running three different legal systems. Each legal system differs from the others and functions differently to meet the needs of a certain group of people in Nigeria.[25] Would a Yoruba woman whose husband is permitted under customary law to marry a second wife consider herself to be discriminated against just because common law does not allow the husband of her Christian friend in the same city to marry a second wife? Of course not. That *the Shari`ah* prescribes a harsher punishment for certain crimes does not amount to discrimination. A man who lives in Texas in America could receive the death penalty if he was convicted of homicide, but another man living in New Jersey would likely receive life imprisonment for exactly the same crime. Can the Texan inmate argue that he has been discriminated against even though both he and the New Jersey man are Americans? Of course not.[26] Justice Agabi's argument implies that there is a unified system of law in Nigeria. He more than anyone knows that there are three systems and that they are all of equal status. Applying the *Shari`ah* to Muslims is not discrimination.

Our understanding of Section 42 (1) (a) is that if any court or judge claims to be applying common law, for instance, the convicted persons under common law should receive equal treatment wherever they reside in Nigeria. They should not be discriminated against in any region in Nigeria. Likewise, the *Shari`ah* should be applied justly and equitably to all Muslims who reside in those states that apply Islamic law. That a person receives the death penalty in a state that adopts capital punishment is not discrimination when compared with a person in another state that does not employ the death penalty who receives life imprisonment for the same crime. Hence the allegation that the application of the *Shari`ah* imposes discriminatory punishment on Muslims, and thus amounts to "flouting the Constitution" is weak. The Constitution approves the establishment of *Shari`ah* courts and *Shari`ah* courts of appeal, and it endorses the application of the penal code, the provisions of which apply only in the north according to Section 315 of the 1999 Constitution.

The governor of Niger State, Alhaji Abdukadir Kure, responded to Agabi, arguing:

> The concern expressed by you on the validity of some of our personalization in the light of the provision of section 42 of the Constitution has prompted us to look once more at the said provisions and our respective laws in order to place the fears thus expressed or identify any inconsistency. With respect, we are unable to see any. Those of our laws, especially the penal legislation relating to theft, adultery, homicide, defamation, intoxication, etc. which have been a subject of heated debates in recent times, were informed by some basic principles expressed and entrenched in our Constitution. These

> principles are contained in Section 4 (7), 5, 6, 38 and the preamble to our Constitution. There is no doubt that the penal legislations are not new and have been tested. Between 1966 and 1999, the Penal Code law [was] applicable in all the Northern States of Nigeria in Section 68 subsection 2 for the infliction of harsh punishment to offenders of the Muslim faith.[27]

It should also be pointed out that the *Shari`ah* courts are not the only ones that apply the penal code. All of the courts in Northern Nigeria—the high courts, magistrates' courts and area courts—whether or not they are presided over by a Muslim (alkali) judge, apply the penal code. Thus the allegation that *Shari`ah* courts inflict harsh punishment on members of the Muslim community was a flawed statement. In fact, none of the courts in the north, including the supreme court, is allowed by law to apply the common criminal law of England. Any appeal from the *Shari`ah* and area courts to the courts of appeal and the supreme courts is adjudicated according to the penal code. It should also be understood that where an area court decides a case according to the *Shari`ah,* then all courts exercising appellate jurisdiction over the case, including the supreme court, are bound by law to apply the *Shari`ah*. This is one of the reasons why, argues Justice Mohammed Bello, under Section 288 of the 1999 Constitution, it is required to have judges in the court of appeal and in the supreme court who are learned in the *Shari`ah*.[28]

From the above analysis we can argue that the application of the *Shari`ah* is constitutional owing to the fact that the Constitution acknowledges the establishment of Islamic courts, including the federal *Shari`ah* Court of Appeal, which receives appeals from the area courts and the *Shari`ah* state courts. Under Section 7 of the Constitution, the state has the power to make laws, including those relating to the *Shari`ah*. Under this power, twelve northern states adopted the *Shari`ah* and penal codes that were endorsed by their State House of Assembly. Section 36 (12) of the Constitution states:

> A person shall not be convicted of a criminal offence unless that offence is defined and the penalty therefore is prescribed in a written law, and in this subsection, a written law refers to an Act of the National Assembly or a Law of a State, any subsidiary legislation or instrument under the provision of a law.

On these grounds the states that apply the *Shari`ah* made sure that their penal codes were passed and adopted by their State House of Assembly. Hence they are not operating any illegal laws; their adjudication is constitutional.

Zamfara State's penal code was adopted by the state house of assembly of Zamfara on January 18, 2000. If such states apply any criminal law which has not been codified or adopted by the National Assembly or the state house of assembly, such an application shall be considered unconstitutional.

It should be pointed out that adopting the *Shari`ah* as an operating legal system in any state does not constitute an adoption of Islam as the state religion, which the Constitution's Section 10 prohibits. The assumption that adopting a criminal code based on a religion carries the same weight as adopting the religion itself is false. If this assumption were true, one would be right to claim that common law or American law is a Christian law, and therefore Christianity is a state religion in Nigeria or America. Common law has its roots in Christianity and is informed by Christian values and its worldviews but it is not a Christian system of law.[29]

On close examination, Islam has not become a state religion in Northern Nigeria, despite the fact that the majority of the population are Muslim. At the same time, it would be unrealistic to assume that the application of the *Shari`ah* would not affect the Christian minority in the north. Christians would definitely be affected in many areas, socially and politically, by the application of the *Shari`ah*. The mere fact that they are in the minority would mean that they would not have a sufficiently loud voice to decide issues affecting all of the citizens in those states that apply the *Shari`ah*. Their rights would be curtailed in some areas, and the application of the *Shari`ah* would definitely affect their businesses, especially those involved in selling alcoholic beverages and promoting gambling.

New *Shari`ah* Cases

Since the adoption of the *Shari`ah* in 2000 a few cases have drawn the attention of the world to Nigeria. More common among these cases are the convictions of Amina Lawal and Safiyatu Husaini. Both were sentenced to death by stoning for adultery, a practice that is illegal. Fortunately, Safiyatu's case has been dismissed for a legal technicality after her appeal to the supreme court, and also partly because of pressure from the world community. People around the world objected to the ruling of stoning on both convicted women on the grounds that the punishment is cruel and that the *Shari`ah* is outdated and should be abandoned because stoning to death for adultery is repugnant to civil society.[30]

The media, both in Nigeria and abroad, has exaggerated these cases without any objectivity by emphasizing the harsh punishment involved in Islamic law. These events in Nigeria give the media and the opponents of the *Shari`ah* an easy opportunity to vent their anger and dissatisfaction about the Islamic legal system, which they know little about. Some call the application of Islamic law the "Talibanization of Nigeria," even though Safiyatu had been sentenced to death before September 11, 2001. Some Nigerians call for the separation of the north from the south by taking up arms, as if the *Shari`ah* had just been launched in 2000 by the Zamfara governor. Unfortunately, the world community danced to that tune by condemning Islam, Muslims and Islamic law in Nigeria. Thus when Safiyatu Husaini's case was dismissed, the thirty-five year old woman received an invitation to move to Rome in Italy. She went and was given a warm welcome, and she was given an honorary award for being freed from the yoke of the *Shari`ah*. Was the award intended to recognize and promote her illegal practice or to condemn the *Shari`ah*, or both? Should the Vatican promote illegal sexual relationships and embrace those who fornicate? The motives of the opponents of the *Shari`ah* are yet to be understood. More will be said about this case and that of Amina Lawal in Chapter 4.

Why Do Northerners Favor the Application of the *Shari`ah*?

There is no easy answer to this question. However, one may surmise that northerners are searching for a unified identity. They want to regain some of their alleged old glories of the unified north. When in 1999 the governor of Zamfara State, Ahmed Sani Yerima, announced that he wanted to apply the *Shari`ah*, it was expected that people would reject his proposal, especially those in Kano and Kaduna, who are perceived as *liberal* owing to their living in the center of commerce in the north. However, it appears that the majority of people in these states were dissatisfied with the secularization, globalization and Westernization that they had witnessed from 1960 until 1999, even though Nigerian leaders during that period came from the north and ruled Nigeria for thirty-one years. They failed to bring peace or harmony to the country because of their corruption, mismanagement and lack of vision. Many scholars from the north attribute the corruption to secular education, which paves ways to Westernization and so led, they assumed, to moral decadence. The leaders paid little attention to moral values as they degraded the role of religion in building Nigerian society. Therefore, rallying around the *Shari`ah* is believed to be an attempt by the northerners to regroup themselves under a religious umbrella—Islam. If it is successful, it would create a great unified power, which the north could exploit politically against the Southerners to win future elections. The majority of northerners believe that it is through the banner of Islam that they can be united. Even though many label the northerners as Hausas, there are many groups in the north, including the Fulanis and the Tivs. Some of these Fulanis and Tivs are also non-Muslims.

Conclusion

The controversy over the application of the *Shari`ah* in Nigeria is not new. However, before anyone can begin blaming Islam and Muslims, it should be noted that the northern states are operating within the 1999 Constitution by adopting the *Shari`ah*. The establishment of the *Shari`ah* does not constitute the adoption of Islam as a state religion, which the Constitution prohibits. Each state has been allowed by the Constitution to establish *Shari`ah courts* to apply Islamic law to meet Muslims' legal needs. I have argued, too, that applying *the Shari`ah* to Muslims does not constitute discrimination against them. Muslims reject the notion that Islamic punishments are hard to bear. They are, without doubt, the majority in the north, and if they desire to be governed by the *Shari`ah*, they should be free to do so, just as any other citizens in Nigeria may ask for their right to apply the law they want. Nigeria, being a secular state, and a republic for that matter, does not prevent her citizens from practicing their beliefs and exercising their religious rights in applying Islamic law as long as they do not enforce it on others. The tension between Muslims and non-Muslims stems from mistrust and suspicion of one another as a result of the long rivalry between Islam and Christianity, and there is no sign that this will end soon.

In my view the application of the *Shari`ah* should not lead to social problems or civil war. *Shari`ah* is a system of law, and the function of law should be to integrate a society through the administration of justice and the legal structure. If the *Shari`ah* can bring peace, justice, harmony, fairness and equal treatment of the citizens to the north, then the Muslim of Northern Nigeria should be free to apply it. Certainly the Constitution endorses three legal systems and this implies that each differs from the others. No group in Nigeria advocates for the unification of all of the legal systems. The diversity of the system is unique and should be perceived as a strength in meeting the needs of Nigerian citizens. In the USA, the most developed country in the world, there are different laws in different states. Texas applies capital punishment to its murderers while many other states in America do not endorse the death penalty. Each state is free to enact whatever law it likes and to apply it as long as the citizens of that state agree to it.

Can the Application of the *Shari`ah* be Stopped?

The expansion of the application of the *Shari`ah* to cover all aspects of life has irritated many Nigerians, including some Muslims. This tension has to be resolved amicably through dialogue between Muslim leaders and the government. All differences between these two parties can be worked out through sincere and genuine dialogue rather than through the courts, or by civil war or separation from the federal government, as suggested by a few Christians from the south. Nigeria should never attempt separation along religious line because this would lead to disaster. No one would benefit from it. We should recognize that Muslims and non-Muslims, Hausas, Yorubas and Ibos are neighbors. No ethnic group would leave its locale or place of residence for another. Hence they are bound to live together peacefully. Separation of each ethnic group will not solve the country's social, religious and political problems. The core of its social problems is not religion but corruption, unfair distribution of the national wealth and lack of patriotism for the country among much of the population.[31] There are many Nigerians abroad in the USA and Europe with high levels of education, but the majority of them prefer to stay abroad rather than return home and make a sacrifice for the country in the way that Indians, Chinese and Israelis do by returning home and building up their country after they receive their education abroad.

We believe that one of the areas of discontent is the application of Islamic criminal laws (***hudud***), especially the stoning to death of an adulterer and the amputation of a thief's hand. Both are subject to reinterpretation. We should point out that while the source of Islamic law is divine for being a revealed law, its application is human. Muslim scholars have a duty to determine how Islamic law should be applied in this contemporary age to ensure that justice and fairness are achieved. The primary aim of the *Shari`ah* in inflicting severe punishment on offenders who commit adultery, theft and armed robbery is to make the punishment a deterrent to potential offenders.[32] This objective can be achieved in various ways. Such an approach to the *Shari`ah* needs an effort from legal scholars and leaders to be realistic, as was the sardauna of Sokoto, Sir Ahmad Bello, in 1956 when he convinced the emirs in Northern Nigeria to accept the provisions of the penal code despite the fact that stoning to death was removed from it. The objective of the *Shari`ah* is not the amputation of a thief's hand but the maintenance of security of all members of the society whereby their properties and lives would be safe.

Muslims and non-Muslims must live together in Nigeria. The issue of the *Shari`ah* will therefore never disappear from Nigerian politics, so this necessitates finding amicable solution to the issue. Condemning its application under any guise of human rights violation or invoking the violation of the Constitution will not help. On the other hand, I believe that the media can do a better job of bringing people together rather than creating sinister and fallacious images of the *Shari`ah*. We should recognize our diversity, appreciate our differences, learn how to communicate with one another with civility and live together peacefully.

Conclusion

Finally, since the beginning of the application of the *Shari`ah* in 2000, we have no enough empirical evidences to substantiate the claim of the Islamists that the social life of the people has improved drastically as a result. Are the people where the *Shari`ah* is applied better off educationally, economically and socially? Are they safer than people living in non-*Shari`ah* states? Are their cities and rural areas more or less developed? Do these states pay adequate attention to educating their citizens and providing sufficient sanitation? These are areas that need more research to assess the benefits of the *Shari`ah* and its accomplishments, if any. I believe that a great deal of attention should be paid to empirical research in these areas if we are to achieve any reliable assessment. If the *Shari`ah* is applied and it does not bring peace and progress to the people, it means it has not been applied properly or it has been abused.

We should realize, too, that there are millions of Muslim Hausas who dwell among the Yorubas and Ibos in Southern Nigeria where the *Shari`ah* is not practiced. These Hausas accommodate their neighbors and hosts, and respect their religions and laws. Thus the Yorubas and Ibos who live in the north should equally respect the Hausas and their religious traditions and beliefs. Nigerians should stop thinking that Hausas are less civilized and that the Yorubas and Ibos are morally responsible to civilize them through Western ways of life or by bringing Christianity to them. The northern Muslims should also refrain from assuming religious superiority by labeling the southerners as *Kafire or Arni* (non-believers). All Nigerians should long for and aspire to industrialization, development and advancement of the whole country. Above all, if the northerners do not want anyone to force Christianity on them under any disguise, they should not force any law on their Christian neighbors under the pretext of applying Islamic law. The population's social, religious and ethnic diversity should be respected and each group should have the freedom to be left alone to determine and practice its religion. If the majority of the people in the north wish to be governed by the *Shari`ah*, as did the twelve states, and they feel satisfied with it, they should be left alone. It is not necessary for all Nigerians to subscribe to a unified legal system. They should cherish their diversity. Even in the USA, each state has its own legal system to meets the needs of the citizens of that particular state. If Nigerians in the south dislike having Islamic law imposed on them, what right do they have to impose Western common law on the Muslims in the North? No legal system is value free. Common law is partly based on Christian and Western values, which have no strong appeal to Muslims in general because of their heavy reliance on materialism, consumerism and secularization. At the same time, Muslims should not impose their law and religious ideas on others in the name of Islam because nothing expressed in the *Qur'an* compels them to do so.[33] Justice and fair play should be the aim of any legislation in Nigeria; it is only through justice and peaceful coexistence that Nigerians can attain peace and live together harmoniously.

Notes

1. Report of the CDC containing the draft constitution for the Federal Republic of Nigeria (Lagos, 1976), sec. 180–186.
2. Salahu-deen Yusuf, "The Press and Islam in Nigeria: A Critical Appraisal of the Impact of Western Press on Some Nigerian Newspaper Media on Issues Relating to Islam and the Muslims," MA thesis, Department. of Islamic Studies, Bayero University, Kano, 1987, p. 67.
3. Ibid., p. 67.
4. Rotimi Williams, "Proceedings of the Constituent Assembly Official Report, Federal Ministry of Information," Lagos, no. Z, November 1, 1977, p. 9.
5. Sam Babs Mala, "The Shari'a and the Treatment of Non-Muslims: A Justified Fear among Nigerians," unpublished manuscript, p. 1.

6. Joseph Kenny is a lecturer in the Department of Religion at the University of Ibadan. He is a missionary working for the establishment of Christianity in Nigeria.
7. Joseph Kenny, "Shari'a in Nigeria: A Historical Survey," in *Bulletin on Islam and Christian-Muslim Relations in Africa* 4 (January, 1986): 1–21.
8. Kenny, "Christian-Muslim Relations in Nigeria," p. 118.
9. Clarke, Peter, *West Africa and Islam*, p. 250.
10. Constitution of the Federal Republic of Nigeria, 1999, sec. 38 (1).
11. Ghazali Basri, *Nigeria and Shari`ah: Aspirations and Apprehensions* (Leicester: The Islamic Foundation, 1994), 43, quoting from the *New Nigerian*, May 8, 1977.
12. Mashood Baderin, "The Shari`ah Alteration: The Moral and Legal Questions," www.nigeriaworld.com, accessed May 5, 2012.
13. Ghazali Basr, *Nigeria and Shari`ah* (Leicester: The Islamic Foundation, 1994), 47–8.
14. Ibid., 48.
15. There is strong evidence that Muslims are in the majority in the north. Any almanac that one consults will state that this is the case. To deny this is to deny a reality. Likewise, Christians are the majority in Eastern Nigeria. There is great controversy as to who is in the majority in Western Nigeria: the Muslims or the Christians? Each group claims to be in the majority. At present there is no conclusive research to support either claim.
16. The governors of those states that apply *Shari`ah* did not stop the application. They asked the chief justice to take the issue to court. However, one of the governors, that of Niger State, Alhaji Kuru, said that the application of *Shari`ah* is constitutional and not discriminatory.
17. T. G. O. Gbadamosi, *The Growth of Islam Among the Yoruba, 1841–1908*, Ibadan History Series (London: Longman, Atlantic Highlands, N. J.: Humanities Press, 1978), p. 233, appendix VI.
18. Mohammed Bello, "Obstacles Before *Sharia*," www.nigeriaworld, posted on February 12, 2002, accessed on May 3, 2012.
19. Area court is the new name given to the former native court. Native court was the name given by the British colonial rulers to the alkali court after the conquest of Sokoto in 1903. The word "native" was used then to neutralize the existing courts, which were Islamic from their religious connotations. The alkali court is a lower court headed by a judge who is learned in Islamic law. Usually the judge in the alkali court decides the cases by himself. The emir court is composed of the emir of the city and a number of people who are learned in Islamic law as assessors. For more information about the history of Islamic law in Nigeria, see Yushau Sodiq, "A History of Islamic Law in Nigeria: Past and Present," *Islamic Studies*, 31 (Spring 1992): 85–108.

20. This case is reported by Alhaji Ma'ji Isa Shani and Mohammad Altaf Hussain Ahangar, "Marriage Guardianship in Islam: Reflections on a Recent Nigeria Judgment," in *Islamic and Comparative Law Quarterly*, 6, no. 4 (1986): 278.
21. Nobody hears much about *Shari`ah* today. Of course, the issue will be raised again in future when circumstances warrant it. At present, little is written or published about *Shari`ah.* In fact the problem facing Nigeria is not that of *Shari`ah* but that of poverty, terrorism, corruption and the unfair distribution of wealth.
22. This is an abuse of the law. However, the law is occasionally abused in Nigeria, be it the *Shari`ah* or common law. Many Nigerians who were in charge of wealth had embezzled (and continue to do so) millions of naira without being brought to justice. It was under Obasanjo that the government began to persecute corrupt civil servants and governors. This is a new beginning that it is hoped will continue. The newly elected President Muhammad Buhari has promised to persecute anyone convicted of corruption and embezzlement.
23. Muhammad Mbahi, "*Sharia*, Northern Ethnic and Religious Minority and the Federal Government: A Perspective," posted at www.nigeriaworld.com, August 10, 2001, accessed on May 3, 2002. At present there is no evidence that the governor had enforced the wearing of a head covering (*hijab*) on his subjects.
24. Justice Godwin Kanu Agabi, "Prohibition of Discriminatory Punishments," a letter written to all twelve states that apply the *Shari`ah* on March 18, 2002. See *Jenda: A Journal of Culture and African Women Studies*, vol. 1&2, 2002. This letter was widely distributed in Nigeria and around the world. Unfortunately the states to which he addressed his letter did not respond, except for Niger and Zamfara states.
25. A perfect example for applying different rules to the same issue is the case of inheritance in Nigeria. The three legal systems in the country have different rules regarding the distribution of wealth from a deceased person.
26. It should be pointed out that Texas is one of the states that endorse capital punishment. More criminals are executed there than in any other state in the USA. Human rights advocates and Amnesty International have objected to capital punishment in Texas but the state legislators always endorse the death penalty. No one argues that the Texans are discriminated against by US law. The country's states have the right to adopt any law they wish. The law represents the will of the people.
27. David Asonye Ihenacho, "The Warped World of the *Sharia* Protagonists," posted on www.nigeriaworld.com/columist/ihenacho/033002, March 30, 2002.

28. Justice Muhammad Bello, "Obstacles Before the *Sharia*," keynote address at the National Seminar on *Shari`ah* in Kaduna on February 10–12, 2000. It is posted on www.nigeriaworld.com on February 12, 2002, accessed on May 3, 2002.
29. Mohammed Haruna, "*Sharia*: Where The Solution Lies," *Today Newspaper*, April 16–22, 2000.
30. I do not think that the appeal court's decision was influenced by the pressure from outside Nigeria. The case of Safiyatu Husaini and Amina Lawal were dismissed on a technical basis as pointed out by the leading defense team for both of them, Aliyu Yawuri.
31. Ben Zwinkels in his recent article on the website AfricaNews mentions that "the Muslim *Sharia* law, which has been introduced in the Northern regions some years ago and which was given a lot of international attention, is now not any more an issue and not anymore always used." The issue, he argues, is about corruption and the increase in poverty for many Nigerians. See www.Africanew.com/site/Ben_Zwinkels, posted on March 3, 2007 accessed on March 11, 2007.
32. The opponents of the *Shari`ah* have argued strongly that the imposition of harsh punishment barely deters criminals from committing crimes. The exponents of the *Shari`ah* argue otherwise and cite the low percentage of crimes in those regions that apply Islamic law, such as Saudi Arabia and even Northern Nigeria. Of course, Saudi Arabia has its own social and political problems.
33. See *Qur'an*, ch 2: 256.

CHAPTER 4

The Structure of the Islamic Courts in Northern Nigeria

Introduction

The real and total application of Islamic law to all spheres of life started with the establishment of the Sokoto Caliphate in 1808 by Shaykh Uthman Dan Fodio. Three types of court emerged: the emir court, the chief alkali court and the alkali court.[1] All of these are still in operation in Northern Nigeria today, with different names. Currently there are native courts, lower courts, upper courts, *Shari`ah* courts and *Shari`ah* Courts of Appeal.

Emir Courts

The emir court is composed of the emir (the mayor) of the locality as the president of that court and a number of persons who are learned in Islamic law as assessors. Usually the emirs are from the descendants or relatives of Dan Fodio; they are expected to be learned in Islamic law. The assessors are appointed by the emirs. This court has the jurisdiction to try any case, including murder and theft. It also has the power to pronounce the death penalty or impose life imprisonment. It has unlimited jurisdiction to try all civil, land and commercial cases as well. Appeals are referred to the emir court from the chief alkali and the alkali courts. All of these courts are *Shari`ah* courts.

Y. Sodiq, *A History of the Application of Islamic Law in Nigeria*,
DOI 10.1007/978-3-319-50600-5_4

The Chief Alkali And Alkali Courts

The chief alkali court is composed of a chief judge and a number of assessors who must be learned in Islamic law. This court has the power to try any case except for murder and land cases, which has to be referred to the emir court. The alkali court is a lower court headed by a judge learned in Islamic law. On several occasions he alone makes decisions. This lower court often tries civil cases that involve punishments that are not prescribed by the *Qur'an* or the *Sunnah*—that is, correctional punishments (*ta'zirat*) on personal matters, family law or cases involving small amounts of money.[2]

It should be noted that, in the past, lawyers were not allowed to represent clients at some *Shari`ah* lower courts on the grounds that they were not eyewitnesses to the events.[3] Anyone who is not satisfied with the procedure at a *Shari`ah* court is free to take his case to the magistrates' court. However, it should also be pointed out that since the 1980s, judges appointed to *Shari`ah* courts are certified judges and lawyers, graduates from Nigerian and overseas universities. Many universities in Nigeria, especially in the north, including Lagos State University, produce graduates with combined law degrees in common law and Islamic law. These graduates must attend Nigerian law school in Lagos before they can be "called to the bar," then they can be appointed as judges after a few years of experience. All *Shari`ah* courts today are under the Ministry of Justice.

Native Courts

When the British occupied Sokoto in 1903, they introduced magistrates' courts which applied English law. The Islamic courts were retained but labeled thereafter as "native courts". The native courts applied Islamic law to Muslims and customary law to non-Muslims.[4] When the native court was established, both the emir and the chief alkali courts lost some of their juridical power. The emir court lost the power to try murder cases and Islamic criminal punishments (*hudud*), such as theft, homicide and adultery.[5]

This situation continued until 1956, when native customary law was enacted in Northern Nigeria.[6] The term "native" was used to neutralize the religious connotation which alkali and emir courts carried. With the introduction of native customary law, native courts ceased to be purely Islamic. The major change in the new law was the substitution of Islamic criminal law by the Penal Code of 1959, which contained some aspects of Islamic offenses with some radical modifications in the prescribed punishments.

The motive behind this substitution was the claim to make the law in Northern Nigeria more suitable for Muslims and non-Muslims.[7] Thus the native courts applied the Native Court Laws of 1956 and followed the magistrates' court procedures. The native courts were classified into different grades. The former emir court became grade A native court unlimited; the chief alkali court became grade B limited, and the alkali courts were classified as grades B, C and D. The jurisdiction of both grades A unlimited and B limited remained as they were in civil matters, although their powers were reduced drastically in criminal issues.[8] The native court grades B, C and D had different jurisdictions that were limited in scope. According to the statistical report, there were 752 native courts in Northern Nigeria as of May 1962. There were 25 grade A unlimited courts, 23 grade A limited, 214 grade B, 261 grade C and 229 grade D.[9] These numbers have changed drastically today. Every state in the north has hundreds of courts with different jurisdictions. Those which do not have *Shari`ah* Courts of Appeal have high magistrates' courts which receive appeals from the lower courts.

Area Courts

The native courts were changed to Area courts through the Area Courts Edict of 1967. Area courts were also classified into grades: upper area court, area court grade I and area court grade II:[10]

1. The upper area court has unlimited power and jurisdiction in civil cases, but limited power in criminal cases. It is bound by the provisions of the criminal procedure code.
2. The area court grade I is proportionally limited in its jurisdiction in civil cases and strictly limited in criminal cases. It cannot impose a prison term of more than three years or a fine of more than 1000 naira.[11]
3. The area court grade II is the lowest court with the most limited jurisdiction. It has unlimited power over matrimonial and custody cases, and many other rules that relate to native law. These courts are subject to the supervision of the high court of the state. The judges in area courts are appointed by the Nigerian public service

commission. The upper area court replaces the former emir and chief alkali's courts. Appeals from area courts grade I and II go to upper area courts; appeals from upper area courts go to the *Shari`ah* Court of Appeal on Islamic issues or to the state high court on any other issues.

The *Shari`ah* Court of Appeal

The *Shari`ah* court of appeal was established in 1960 to replace the Moslem court of appeal. It hears appeals from the upper area courts on matters relating to Islamic personal laws[12] that are primarily based on Maliki law.[13] It has its own constitution, which spells out the function of the court, the scope of its jurisdiction, and the procedures and rules to be followed. The composition of judges and the qualifications required of members of the *Shari`ah* court are also explained. Appeals from the *Shari`ah* Court of Appeal go to the Federal Court of Appeal for final decisions.

The Federal Court of Appeal

The Federal Court of Appeal is also a superior court established by the Nigerian military government in 1976.[14] It hears appeals from the State High Courts, the federal revenue courts, the *Shari`ah* Court of Appeal and any other courts specified by the law. It has jurisdiction throughout the country and receives appeals from the entire country. Conclusively, in the cases cited in this work, references are made to the area courts, upper area courts, the *Shari`ah* court of appeal and the federal court of appeal.

It is pertinent to mention here that in Nigeria some judges at the *Shari`ah* courts (especially the elder judges) rely heavily on, for example, *Mukhtasar al-Khalil*[15] and its commentary as the most important textbooks of law. Although *Mukhtasar al-Khalil* is widely read among judges, little attention is paid to such original sources as *al-Muwatta'* of Imam Malik or *al-Mudawwanah al-Kubrah* of Imam Sahnun (a student of Imam Malik). Also, judges rarely quote the *Qur'an* or the *hadith*, which are the primary sources of Islamic law. Instead they cite the authority of Maliki's jurists in any Maliki book and assume that whatever is said therein is authoritative. One wonders why they always resort to secondary Maliki law books rather than to the original sources. No clear reason has been given as to why judges in *Shari`ah* courts often quote authorities from these books, even though those opinions represent only the authors' views or render solutions only for the problems of their time. Although a researcher could find some valuable decisions in those books, some of the verdicts appear to be socially conditioned or outdated, so they may need reinterpretation in the light of today's challenges. I would suggest that the authority of these books be limited and that the general purpose and goal of Islamic law should be given precedence because the opinions of past generations of Muslim scholars may be irrelevant and serve no benefit for today's Muslims. It is key to keep in mind the spirit of Islam, whose laws are intended to maintain justice, fair treatment and peace for all humanity.

In the following I shall cite a few cases of how Islamic law is applied in Islamic courts and how judges have reached their conclusions. In addition, where the parties did not accept the judgments of the court, they appealed to a higher court up to the Federal Court of Appeal in Kaduna or Lagos. The judgment of the latter is the final judgment which all parties had to accept. I choose the following cases to show that the *Shari`ah* in Nigeria is not static and is always subject to interpretation by the judges, and that if anyone disagrees with the verdict of any Islamic court they can take their case to any other superior court up to the Federal Court of Appeal.

Case One: The Right of a Female to Marry Whom She Wants

Introduction to the Case

The status of women in Islam has undergone many stages of reform and development. When Islam was established by the Prophet Muhammad in the seventh century, a number of reforms were introduced. For the first time in Arabia, women were free to marry whomever they chose. The marriage contract was no longer between the groom and the bride's father but between the groom and the bride.[16] Women became real participants; they had the right to say no and to determine the content of their marriage contract as granted to them by the Prophet.

Women enjoyed these liberties from the time of the Prophet until the decline of the Muslim world in the thirteenth century, when women's role and rights began to be undermined.[17] Islamic marriage, which was intended to be a contract between two people—wife and husband—became a contract between parents and guardians. Women were seen as commodities and thus had no choice in their marriage. Minor marriages were encouraged, and the liberty to accept or reject an offer was denied.

And since many women were uneducated, they were ignorant of their rights. They became victims of the patriarchic society which did not respect them at all. As time went on, polygamous marriages and divorce rates increased, and androcentric ideology took root. This continued until the beginning of the twenty-first century.[18] Today there are many Muslim women [in some Muslim countries] who are forced to marry their relatives against their will. Even though the Islamic courts continue to rescue the situation, the culture exerts great pressure on couples to accept the decisions of their parents. While this "arranged marriage" may have some limited merit, its evils override its advantages. Some women today are bold enough to reject arranged marriage but a few still accept it, claiming that they have no choice, whereas the religion of Islam gives them the choice to say "No." as endorsed by the Prophet.

After the fall of the Ottoman Empire in 1922 and the abolition of the Islamic caliphate by Mustafa Kamal Ataturk in 1924, the Muslim world witnessed a pseudo-reform which included the reconstruction of Islamic family law. In a number of Muslim countries (e.g. Egypt, Syria, Morocco, and Jordan), polygamy was brought under control. In some others (e.g. Algeria and Tunisia), it has been banned. Minor marriages have also been combated, and marriages without consent are constantly checked by the law. However, in many Muslim countries, arranged marriages continue, including in some part of Northern Nigeria and in Kwara State in Yorubaland.

My research shows that Nigeria is not practically affected by these new trends in marriage reform. No reforms have been carried out publicly either by Muslim leaders or by women. Of course, there are a few cases where women have made bold attempts to let their voices be heard, calling for the attention of the public to their problems.[19] One such event is the case of Karimatu Yakubu. The question is, what is the status of Muslim women in particular and all Nigerian women in general in the twenty-first century? Are they free to marry who they want? Do they stay silent? Karimatu's case[20] may appear strange to a Western audience, but arranged marriages are common in many cultures in Africa, Asia and Arabia. What is strange, in my view, is using Islam to justify its continued practice. My research on Islam shows that arranged marriage is a cultural phenomenon that has been introduced into Islam. It is not encouraged by the Prophet; it has no basis in the *Qur'an* and in the authentic *Sunnah* of the Prophet. He objected to this idea completely and encouraged parents to allow their daughters to marry whom they choose because they rather than their parents are the ones who have to live with their husband. Marriage should be based on love. Of course, parents can offer valuable advice but they should not allow their daughter to marry a man she doesn't love.

Karimatu Yakubu and Alhaji Mahmoud Ndatsu v. Alhaji Yakubu Tafida Paiko and Alhaji Umaru Gwagwada

In this case Karimatu Yakubu and Alhaji Mahmoud Ndatsu were the appellants. Two legal issues were involved:

1. Does a daughter have the right to choose whom to marry, or does her father have the right to force her to marry whom he chooses?
2. If a father voluntarily initially allows his daughter to choose her husband, can he withdraw his permission and thus prevent her from choosing whom she wants?

I shall describe the case as it was reported, explain how the *Shari`ah* court judges made their decisions and analyze the assumptions behind their judgments in the light of the *Qur'an* and the *Sunnah*. My aim is to determine whether or not a young Muslim woman has the right "Islamically" to choose her husband. Karimatu is a daughter of Alhaji Yakubu Tafida Paiko. At the age of nineteen, three suitors wanted to marry her and her father rejected one of them.[21] He informed her about the other two—Alhaji Mahmoud Ndatsu and Alhaji Umaru Gwagwada[22]—and allowed her to choose between them. Karimatu was inclined initially to marry Alhaji Umaru based on information that she had heard about him, although she did not meet him. Her father wanted her to marry Alhaji Mahmoud,[23] so he allowed Mahmoud to meet her with the hope that he might win her heart.

However, Karimatu preferred Alhaji Umaru, who subsequently sent a message of betrothal to which the father agreed. Before the marriage ceremony was solemnized officially, Karimatu changed her mind. She complained that Umaru did not visit her after their first meeting but continuously sent a middleman instead. She interpreted his attitude as a lack of love and concern for her at that very crucial stage and thus declined to marry him. At that time she was away from her home town. Now she preferred Alhaji Mahmoud instead. She wrote to her father and her uncle explaining to them the reason why she had changed her mind. Her choice received a bitter response from her father, who wanted her to marry Alhaji Umaru because he had said yes to him.[24] When she could not convince her father of her new choice, she wrote to her uncle and to the chief judge of Sokoto State, seeking their advice.[25]

Before she received a response, things got out of control: in her absence her father had conducted a marriage on her behalf to Alhaji Umaru. She did not agree to it and refused to go to Umaru. She then sued her father in the area court in Minna in Niger State where she was studying. After the court had examined the case, it dissolved her marriage on the grounds that she was married to him without her consent. Based on that judgment, she married Alhaji Mahmoud, whom she had chosen instead. The emir of Minna acted as her guardian instead of her father,[26] who refused to be her guardian in this second marriage.[27]

Karimatu's father disagreed with the area court's decision and he appealed to the *Shari`ah* court of appeal in Sokoto. The judges there accepted his appeal and confirmed the father's right to force his daughter into a marriage without her consent.[28] The court reversed the decision of the area court and ordered Karimatu to leave Alhaji Mahmoud's house, observe the legal term of abstinence (*'iddah*)[29] and move to Alhaji Umaru's residence. The judges argued that there was no reason why the father should be deprived of his right of compulsion (*ijbar*) in marriage.

Alhaji Mahmoud, Karimatu's second husband, did not accept the *Shari`ah* Court of Appeal's judgment. He appealed to the federal court of appeal in Kaduna. After hearing from both sides, the federal court of appeal endorsed the decision of the area court and set aside the judgment of the *Shari`ah* court of appeal, but on different grounds: it judged that Karimatu's marriage to Mahmoud was legitimate and that she should stay with him. Her choice of marriage should be respected. That was the final judgment, thus Karimatu remained as Alhaji Mahmoud's wife.

A Synopsis of the Arguments Relied upon by Each Court in Making Its Decision

The Area Court at Minna

The area court dissolved the marriage between Karimatu and Alhaji Umaru because the marriage was conducted on her behalf without her consent.[30] Therefore one important feature of the marriage contract in Islam had been violated, which rendered the contract invalid. It appears that the judges in the area court did not recognize the right of compulsion (*ijbar*) in marriage as claimed by the Maliki school. Another factor that might have influenced the decision is that because Karimatu's father allowed her in the beginning to choose whom she liked, that permission could not be withdrawn, so her choice had to be respected.[31] And if she could exercise it the first time, she should be allowed to exercise it the second time and more.

The Shari`ah Court of Appeal at Sokoto

The grounds on which the *Shari`ah* Court of Appeal based its decision

The judges at the *Shari`ah* court of appeal confirmed that the father had a right to compel his daughter to marry whomever he chose for her. The court observed that:

> Under the strict interpretation of the law according to the Maliki School, a father has the right to marry his virgin daughter without seeking her consent, irrespective of her age; but if he wishes, he may consult her.[32]

Relying on this statement, the court insisted that the father must be given the opportunity to exercise his right, regardless of any consequence of his decision on the daughter.

The Federal Court of Appeal at Kaduna

The grounds on which the Federal Court of Appeal based its judgment

The federal court of appeal[33] argued that the father had the right to compel his daughter to marry whomever he chooses for her without her consent if she is a minor. However, because he had given her the freedom to choose, his right was forfeited. In its decision to allow the appeal and to nullify the *Shari`ah* court of appeal's judgment, the judges at the federal court of appeal observed that:[34]

> Secondly, where a father has given his virgin daughter the right to choose between her two or more suitors, he has lost his power of compulsion (*ijbar*), and any marriage conducted without her consent is invalid. Consequently, the marriage of the first appellant [Karimatu] to the second respondent [Alhaji Umaru] by the first respondent [Alhaji Paiko] is void.

Discussion of the Arguments

There are three arguments here:

1. The consent of a would-be wife constitutes a fundamental condition in Islamic marriage. Without the consent of both parties, no marriage is valid.

2. Maliki law confers on a father the right to compel his virgin daughter to marry whom he chooses without her consent. This right should be respected.
3. The right of compulsion (*ijbar*) ceases to be an exclusive and absolute right of the father whenever he voluntarily gives this right away by allowing his daughter to exercise it.

I will discuss these arguments individually and examine whether or not they are admissible and legitimate in court.

The Necessity for Consent in Marriage

Is the consent of the bride a necessity in an Islamic marriage? According to the *hadith*,[35] it is both necessary and crucial. Failure to obtain it will render the marriage void. Her consent may be known through her expressed words or her reaction after she has been informed about a suitor. She may even convey her intention by keeping silent. The following are some of the sayings of the Prophet Muhammad (in the *hadith*) concerning consent in marriage:

1. Abu Hurayrah reported that the Prophet said:[36]

> The widow and the divorced women shall not be married until their permissions are obtained, and the virgin (*bikr*) shall not be married until her consent is obtained. They (the companions) asked, how could we know her consent? He answered, by her silence.

2. Ibn Abbas reported that:[37]

> Once, a young woman came to the Prophet, may the peace of Allah be upon him, and complained that her father gave her in marriage (to somebody) and she objected to that. The Prophet gave her a choice (either to stay with him or to nullify the marriage).

These *hadith* establish that the consent of daughters must be obtained in marriage. In addition, all Islamic schools of law consider the consent of the bride and bridegroom to be the foremost condition in marriage. This is what Muslim jurists termed as 'offer and acceptance' (*ijab*) and (*qabul*).[38] They unanimously affirm that any marriage that lacks this condition is invalid.

In *al-Muwatta'*, Imam Malik reported that the Prophet ordered that the consent of a virgin woman be obtained before giving her in marriage, and if she did not give an expressed consent, her silence would be regarded as an indication of approval.[39] This *hadith* shows that she must be informed of any suitor who seeks her hand in marriage, and she must be allowed to express herself. If enough time is given to her and she does not raise any objection, her silence is considered as her approval.

Imam Malik also explained the practice of the people of Medina and reported that some companions, such as Qasim ibn Muhammad and Salam ibn 'Abd Allah, used to choose husbands for their daughters without seeking their daughters' permission.[40] However, that practice was not in accord with the Prophet's sayings. According to Imam Malik's principle, when there is a conflict of opinion between the Prophet's saying and the companions' practices, the Prophet's authentic saying should be given preference.

On the other hand, Muslim jurists regard marriage as a social contract (*aqd*) as well as a religious duty. As a contract, marriage is not legally valid without the consent of both parties.[41] The often cited case of A'ishat, in which the Prophet Muhammad married her at the age of nine with the permission of her father, was rejected by Imam Ibn Hazm al-Zahiri,[42] who insisted that the Prophet married her with her permission.

The conclusion that can be drawn from the above discussion is that seeking the consent of the bride is requested in Islamic marriage as expressed by the Prophet Muhammad.[43] Because this was important, the Prophet gave the woman who came to him complaining about her father a choice to accept what her father had done or to reject the marriage.[44] The practice of some companions could be explained by saying that they acted in this way because they knew that their daughters would consent to whatever they decided. Since there were no such reports of objection from those daughters, the implication was that they endorsed their fathers' choices. However, this tendency among the companions should not lead Muslims to underrate the importance of seeking the consent of their daughters before giving them in marriage. In practice, the Prophet's request indicates the invalidity of any marriage that lacks the consent of the woman.

If this conclusion is acceptable, its application to the case of *Karimatu Paiko v. Alhaji Paiko and Alhaji Umaru* would suggest that the first marriage concluded by Alhaji Paiko without the consent of Karimatu was 'invalid' in Islam.[45] There was an offer from Umaru but no acceptance from Karimatu at the time of marriage, thus the contract was incomplete and the marriage was void. Karimatu had proved to her father her lack of interest by arguing that Alhaji Umaru showed no concern for her by not meeting her. In this marriage, Karimatu was convinced that her father was not safeguarding her interests. Certainly it seems that the behavior of her father did not meet the required conditions. He acted according to the local [unIslamic] custom of occasionally disregarding women's opinions in marriage owing to the patriarchal structure of the society, especially among the Hausas.

The Father's Right of Compulsion

Does a father have a right to compel his daughter in marriage without her consent in Maliki law? The report from Imam Malik is not helpful here if one considers the context in which that opinion was expressed. In *al-Mudawwanah al-Kubra*, Sahnun[46] said to Ibn al-Qasim:[47]

> Suppose she [a daughter] rejected the suitors one after another, should she be forced to marry? Ibn al-Qasim answered, she should not be compelled to marry according to Malik. No one should force another to marry except the father, who can compel his virgin daughter, his children, male or female. A guardian may also exercise this right over an orphan. Ibn al-Qasim said, certainly, a person asked Malik and I was present that he had a daughter of his brother who was immature (*safih*). The man wanted to give her in marriage to somebody who could protect her and preserve her but she objected. Malik responded, she should not be married without her consent. The man said, she was immature; she acted stupidly in her affairs. Malik answered, even if she was stupid, he had no right to give her in marriage without her consent.

In this quotation, it appears that the daughter had rejected many suitors, and Imam Malik insisted that she should not be compelled to marry without her consent. However, if she rejected all suitors or had no interest in marriage, she might be strongly encouraged by her father to marry. Even if we interpret Malik's statement "no one should force another to marry except the father" as permission for a father to force his daughter to marry, it would be an exceptional case and should not be regarded as a rule to be followed in all cases. The context of the discussion shows that a daughter might be compelled only if she had rejected many offers and she insisted that she did not want to marry.[48] Then her rejection might be caused by her lack of experience in identifying the best suitor. In such a situation, she might need assistance from her father or a guardian. Such interference from the father would be dictated by the daughter's condition.

Nevertheless, the consent of the daughter is obviously essential. This appeared vividly in Imam Malik's response to the person who wanted to give his brother's daughter in marriage because he thought she was immature. Malik insisted that she must agree to the marriage, otherwise no marriage should be conducted. It might also be mentioned that the above quote from *al-Mudawwanah* is the only original text ascribed to Imam Malik by Ibn Al-Qasim regarding the right of a father to compel his daughter in marriage.[49] The judges in Nigeria hardly make no reference to this original source. Instead they refer to other sources, such as *Mukhtasar al-Khalil* and *Kitab al-Tuhfah*, both of which are law textbooks used in Nigeria.

The above extract from Malik also suggests that the father is at times allowed to interfere and influence his daughter's opinions. However, he did not confer any right on the father. In Islam, only God and his Prophet can confer on the father the right to compel or not. Hence what Malik said was his opinion, and it should not be taken as a final authority, such as the content of the *Qur'an* or a commandment from the Prophet Muhammad.

As stated in the *hadith,* the Prophet did not give the fathers a legal right to force their daughters to marry. Rather, he emphasized that the daughters' consent must be obtained.[50] Therefore there is no sufficient and convincing reason for Alhaji Paiko and the judges in the *Shari`ah* Court of Appeal to argue that he had a right to marry his daughter to whomever he wanted without her consent.

On the other hand, Ibn al-Qasim's report in *al-Mudawwanah* mirrors only Imam Malik's opinion in consideration of the daughter's interests. However, in Karimatu's case, it appears that her father was not acting in her best interests.[51] Perhaps it is against her interests to be married to somebody she does not know or like, or to be married before she understands what marriage involves. In the *hadith* the Prophet said, "A father should seek the permission of his virgin daughter before giving her in marriage to another."[52] He also said, "When a man gives his daughter in marriage and she dislikes it, the marriage shall be repudiated."[53]

All these *hadith* confirm my opinion that a woman has the choice to accept or reject any suitor her father presents to her. Because she must live with the man, she must be given the chance to select whomever she likes and loves. Thus I conclude that no father has the right to compel his daughter into marriage because it is against the expressed text in the *hadith* and the spirit of Islam. It is through legitimate marriage that the family is composed in Islam and therefore it should be established on the principles of love, affection and peace.

It should also be noted that compulsion may apply only when a woman cannot decide for herself for some reason.[54] In the above case, Karimatu seems to be a mature girl who knows what marriage is; she recognizes that she must live with her husband. Thus to force her to marry without her consent would be an intrusion on her freedom. She fought for her freedom of choice and she won it.

Forfeit of the Power of Compulsion Through the Father's Permission for His Daughter to Choose

If the argument that the father has no right of compulsion is acceptable, the question of whether he can withdraw his permission will not arise. Because he has no right initially, there is nothing to be withdrawn. Thus the decision of the Federal Court of Appeal that because Karimatu's father had allowed her to make a choice he could not withdraw from it has no basis, in my view. If his right cannot be established legally, he cannot exercise it, hence there is nothing to be withdrawn. Islamic marriage is based on four elements: the consent of both parties (husband and wife); the giving of a dowry to the wife; the approval of the guardian; and the marriage contract being enacted in the presence of two witnesses.

In conclusion, the guardian, whether he is the father or someone else, is supposed to safeguard the daughter's interests. Karimatu's father appeared to have little interest in his daughter's concern and welfare, thus the area court's judges ruled that he did not deserve to be a guardian. Imam Malik was reported to have deprived a father of being a guardian when that father disregarded his daughter's interests.[55] Malik allowed somebody else to be the guardian instead.[56] Therefore the decision by the *Shari`ah* court of appeal was not based on the expressed text of the *hadith*, neither was it based on *Maslahah* [the consideration of the public good]. Rather, the *Shari`ah* court of appeal inclined to the view expressed in Maliki legal books regardless of whether that view served the interests of the parties involved or whether it promoted justice and fair dealing. The claim that the father should be given the right of compulsion, perhaps on the basis of *maslahah*, ceases to be applicable here because he lacked an interest in his daughter's choice.

The federal court of appeal based its judgment on a weak source by relying on the precedent of the case of *Baiwa v. Alhaji Isa Bida*[57] rather than on the original source[58] from which the *Shari`ah* Court of Appeal derived its judgments. The foundation on which the area court based its judgment—the need for the consent of the woman—is strong and essential. Unfortunately it was neglected by both the *Shari`ah* Court of Appeal and the federal court of appeal.

On the other hand, this case proves that the *Shari`ah* Court of Appeal occasionally overlooks the dynamism of Islamic law and overcharges the cultural and social elements that led to the verdicts given in some Maliki law books, such as *al-Risalah* of Shaykh Qayrawan or *Mukhtasar al-Khalil.* As shown in some cases I collected in Nigeria, in most cases the *Shari`ah* courts apply the laws as contained in the legal textbooks and hardly make reference to the *Qur'an* and the *hadith*, except on rare occasions.[59] At time this has led to an abuse of the application of Islamic law in Nigeria. Women should be free to choose their husbands and parents should limit their role to an advisory status. Islam requires only that a Muslim woman marries a Muslim man, and that she chooses an equal to herself, somebody she loves and would like to live with peacefully.

Case Two: A Wife's Right To Divorce Her Husband

Introduction to the Case

In Islam a woman has the right to divorce her husband, just as a man has the right to divorce his wife. Marriage in Islam is a contract which each party enters into freely and can leave freely. While men often exercise this right, women hardly do because they see themselves as being deprived of their rights by the patriarchal society through the pressure placed on them by men.

The Maliki law recognizes three kinds of dissolution of marriage: regular divorce (*talaq*), divorce through compensation (*Khulu`*) and dissolution by the court (*al-Talaq minal Qadi*). In a regular divorce (*talaq*) the husband has the right to divorce his wife for genuine reasons.[60] Unfortunately, Muslim men in Nigeria sometimes abuse this privilege by divorcing their wives without proper cause or good reason.[61] When the husband initiates divorce, he receives nothing from what he had given to her as a dowry (*mahr*). This form of divorce has been recognized by Muslim jurists in all four Sunni schools of law, and the law governing it is clearly expressed in the *Qur'an*[62] and the *Sunnah.*

Divorce through compensation (*Khulu`*) is initiated by the wife. The law requires that the wife refunds to the husband what she received as a dowry during the marriage contract. Usually the husband still has some interest in his wife but she loses interest in him. Thus she compensates for his loss, or at least she returns to him what he had invested in her materially. This form of divorce is also recognized in all schools .[63]

In the third type, the court separates the couple because of maltreatment or the husband's inability to provide maintenance for his wife. The husband may or may not agree to the court's decision, and he may or may not receive any compensation from his wife. Here the wife is forced to seek separation for some reason. The court interferes to stop the injustice and dispute when the marriage can no longer be maintained peacefully. The Maliki and Hanbali jurists recognize this form of separation,[64] but some Hanafi and Shafi'i scholars object to it.[65] The following case is an example of a dissolution in which the husband did not receive the dowry money that he had paid to his wife, and she was set free by the court. The husband was even punished for his cruelty to her.

Hasana Gbaguda v. Muhammadu Gbaguda

In this case,[66] Hasana Gbaguda, the appellant, sued her husband Muhammadu Gbaguda. She filed for divorce at Bida upper area court in Niger State and charged the respondent with mistreatment. She claimed that he beat her several times when he got drunk. The husband admitted the charges but asked the court not to separate them. Despite his confession of drinking and beating his wife,[67] the court ordered the wife to return to her matrimonial home. It argued that she had no right to divorce her husband. If she still wanted separation from him, it should be through *Khulu`*,[68] whereby she had to return the dowry that she had received during her marriage to him. Hasana was returned to Gbaguda's house by force (with the aid of the police) in compliance with the court's decision. After some time, she went back to the court and paid 160 naira as *Khulu`*. Although the court received the money and paid it to Muhammadu Gbaguda, still Hasana was not released from the marriage as indicated in the court's report.[69]

Unsatisfied with the area court's silence and inaction, she appealed to the *Shari`ah* Court of Appeal, begging it to dissolve her marriage with Muhammadu Gbaguda. Her appeal rested on three points:

1. Her husband was a drunkard, and she did not want to live with him anymore.
2. He often beat her.

3. The area court in Bida used force to return her to Gbaguda's house despite Gbaguda's confession of maltreatment and drinking.

The *Shari`ah* Court of Appeal summoned both parties and sought evidence from them. The husband admitted the charges of beating and drinking but claimed that his wife was seeking a *Khulu`* divorce. He admitted that he had taken the *Khulu`* money from the area court but did not let her go. After deliberation, the *Shari`ah* court of appeal decided that the wife should be separated from her husband because she was abused, beaten and molested. It ordered that the husband pay back to her the sum of 160 naira. He was also punished for maltreatment of his wife. The court argued that the husband did not deserve the money or any other compensation because he caused the divorce through his cruel manner and inhumane treatment of his wife.

The Analysis of the Case

Two things are involved in this case: the grounds on which the *Shari`ah* court based its decision and the underlying assumption of that judgment. First, the judge referred to the book *Mawahib al-Khalil, Sharh Mukhtasa al-Khalil.* The author states that the court has the authority to dissolve a marriage in which a father marries his daughter to a drunkard[70] because the husband cannot be trusted and can do whatever he wants with his wife when he is under the influence of alcohol. The author claims that to prevent such occurrences the law allows separation if the wife shows no interest in continuing to live with her husband.

I think that separation because of mistreatment was based on *maslahah*, which is seeking the interests of the bride, protecting her from destruction and safeguarding the peace of the community. In addition, the decision of the *Shari`ah* Court of Appeal confirms that the Maliki school recognizes the wife's right to procure a divorce in practice because of maltreatment or lack of maintenance. The *Shari`ah* courts in Nigeria allow women to enjoy this right.[71]

Another important issue is the return of the compensation money (*Khulu`*) to the wife. Usually, whenever a wife asks for a divorce, she pays back what she receives from her husband.[72] In this case the *Shari`ah* court of appeal ordered the refund of what the husband received from the wife, arguing that he did not deserve such reimbursement. The court also referred to *Al-Fawakih al-Dawaani*, which states:

> If there has been cruelty such as beating and the use of abusive language, then the wife is entitled to *Khulu`*, and the *Khulu`* divorce still stands.[73]

Theoretically the Maliki jurists allow divorce on the grounds of maltreatment, and this case exemplifies the practical aspect of that theoretical opinion. This case is one of the rare examples of a *Khulu`* divorce where the wife got back what she had paid to the husband. The court's decision does not accord with the Prophet's judgment regarding the wife of Thabit ibn Qays, but it concurs with the objectives of Islamic law,[74] which is the protection of the family, bringing peace to the community and allowing the woman the right not to stay with an abusive husband.

To what extent did the *Shari`ah* court of appeal's decision correspond to the spirit of Islam? Usually in a *Khulu`* divorce the wife returns to the husband what he gave to her as a dowry. There are numerous cases of this. I think that the purpose of *Khulu`* is to offer the wife a legal right to relieve herself from an unexpected experience in marital life, and to compensate the husband by paying back his dowry, in part or in full, so that he does not suffer materially from separation. In either case the wife and the husband are both winners.

The above case conforms to the spirit of Islam in that the separation was intended to end the problem faced by both parties. In addition, asking the husband to return what he took from his wife as *Khulu`* was to teach him the lesson that the wife did not wrong him; rather, his behavior encouraged her to leave him. Apparently the *Shari`ah* court of appeal's decision conforms with the spirit of *Shari`ah* in that it afforded justice to both parties. The judges did not adhere to the letter of the law as contained in the *hadith* but to its spirit, which is the exercise of justice and fair treatment.

In conclusion, it seems that the *Shari`ah* Court of Appeal handled the case fairly and based its decision on what was in the best interest of the people. This is one of the cases that I found where a woman procured divorce and the husband was ordered to refund what she had paid him.

Case Three: Seeking Divorce by the Wife and the *Shari`ah* Court's Disapproval of It

This case was *Habiba Sarkin Fulani v. and Alhaji Dahiru Dayi*. The hearing took place in the *Shari`ah* Court of Appeal in Bauchi State on January 26, 1978.

Habiba Sarkin Fulani sued her husband Alhaji Dahiru Dayi in the area court, alleging that he divorced her. Alhaji Dahiru denied her claim. The wife failed to establish her claim as a result of lack of evidence and reliable witnesses. Hence the area court, which is a lower court, dismissed her case but she was not satisfied. The court advised her to return to her matrimonial home but she refused. When she vowed that she would never return to Alhaji Dahiru's house, he offered to divorce her if she would pay him back the dowry of 500 naira. She agreed to pay. When the money was brought to the court at the next meeting, Alhaji Dahiru had changed his mind and appealed to the court to return Habiba to his home. He refused to take the money, which was then deposited in the bank, but the court passed a decree of judicial divorce on the grounds of *Khulu`* (a divorce by paying the dowry back to the husband).

Alhaji appealed to the upper area court and the latter reversed the decision of the lower court for two reasons, asking the wife her to return to her husband. The first reason for accepting Alhaji Dahiru's appeal was that the court interfered in the question of *Khulu`* between the couple. The second reason was the lower court's failure to quote authoritative references to support its judgment on the issue of *Khulu`*. This upper area court at Galambi in Bauchi State judged that Alhaji Dahiru received his wife back because he did not accept the offer of *Khulu`* even though he was the one who initiated it. Habiba did not accept the decision of this upper court and thus she appealed to the *Shari`ah* court of appeal but the appeal was not granted.

The *Shari`ah* court of appeal held that;

1. When divorce through *Khulu`* is an issue, the duty of the court is to examine the nature and mode of the husband's request for payment of *Khulu`* money.
2. A statement or promise by the husband to accept *Khulu`* money or to divorce his wife on the grounds of *Khulu`* may be binding where contractual relations can be inferred from the circumstances or where the wife is put at a disadvantage.

The appellant, Habiba Sarkin Fulani, contested her case with the respondent, Alhaji Dahiru Dasat, at the Galambi area court on the issue of divorce on the payment of 500 naira as *Khulu`*. Alhaji Dahiru was not satisfied with the decision of the area court so he appealed to the upper area court where the decision of the previous court was dismissed and the subsistence of the marriage was affirmed. The appellant in this case did not accept the decision of the upper area court and so appealed to this *Shari`ah* court, arguing that she had already purchased her freedom by the repayment of the dowry, and that she had even completed her waiting period (*iddah*). Alhaji Dahiru also mentioned that a messenger of the lower court named Buba was sent to him to inform him that his wife would be returned to him.

After hearing the submission of the respondent and going through the copy of the judgment of the trial, the *Shari`ah* court restated the facts as follows:

> As far as we are concerned [the *Shari`ah* Court of Appeal] the issue of the trial judge sending his servant, Buba to the respondent which was brought up at the Upper Area court and at this court, is not something that should come into this case at all. This is due to the uncertainty in the truth of the information. Alhaji Dahiru is an adult and sane and if simply because somebody asked him to divorce his wife, he proceeded to do so, without any intimidation or threat, the divorce will definitely be effective. The only relevant issue to consider in the case is the issue of *Khulu`* so as to see whether it is exactly the type of *Khulu`* on the grounds of which the *Shari`ah* dissolves a marriage or not. We have already seen what Alhaji Dahiru said, "since she said she does not love me—she should pay *Khulu`* to me." Again he later said, "We have decided on the N500 *Khulu`* let her pay me and get released". Habiba brought the N500 to the court the following day, but Alhaji refused to accept the money on the ground[s] that he'd not agree to the *Khulu`*. Here before this court we asked Habiba how she managed to get the money to which she replied that it was given to her by her brother Musa. In Dasuki's commentary on *mukhtasar al Khalil*,[75] Dasuki said: "If a person said to his wife. 'If you give me 1000 Dhirhams I have divorced you or I'll divorce you.' And if she brings the money what should be considered is the nature of what he says. If he says, 'If you give me so much I have divorced you,' and she gave him the amount, the divorce is confirmed, because he has already bound himself. But if he says, 'If you give me so much I'll *consider* divorcing you,' this amounts only to a mere promise which he cannot be forced to fulfill unless it is noticed that much inconvenience is caused on the wife like selling her property before she gets the money. Here the court will force him to fulfill his promise because of the suffering she incurred. But production of the amount he mentioned by the wife will not make his promise binding on him."
>
> There is also the same comment in *'Juwahir al-Iklil*, a commentary on *Mukktasar* (ch 1 p. 336), [76] and also in Al-Sahnu's commentary on *'Zarqani* (ch 4, p. 73). Therefore what we are going to consider in the light of the

above authorities is the nature and mode in which Alhaji Dahiru requested the payment of *Khulu`*. According to the judgment, his statement was, "We have arrived at the decision on *Khulu`* of N500 let her pay me and get released." He did not say, "If she gives me N500 I'll divorce her," but "Let her pay me and get released (divorce). In this situation we are going to consider his statement as a mere promise to divorce her, a promise which did not cause her any inconvenience or sufferings because the money was just given to her by her brother Musa. Since this is the case, Alhaji Dahiru will not be forced to accept or divorce his wife. Because of these reasons we (the judges at the *Shari`ah Court*) are of the opinion that this marriage of Alhaji Dahiru and Habiba is not dissolved on the actual ground of *Khulu`* as recognized by the *Shari`ah*. Finally, we are hereby confirming the decision of the Upper Area court Bauchi and accordingly dismissing the appeal of Habiba.

Analysis of Case 3

It is interesting to note that this case also pertains to divorce through *Khulu` Khulu`*. However, this time the wife's request was not granted because she could not prove anything negative against her husband. She did not charge him with any maltreatment or abuse but just said that she did not like him anymore. Initially she claimed that he had divorced her but she could not prove it. When her husband accidentally voiced his readiness to let her go, she jumped on it but the husband withdrew his consent and insisted that he wanted her back in his home. Despite that she brought the amount he suggested for her release, then he changed his mind and refused to let her go. In my opinion the decision of the upper area court and the *Shari`ah* court of appeal was unacceptable; it did not represent the spirit of Islam. Divorce in Islam is intended to put an end to a marriage which is no longer healthy or functioning. If the wife no longer likes the husband, the relationship will not be cordial and tension will soon grow between them. Even though what the court decided is legally right, it defeats the purpose of marital life, which is the establishment of harmony, peace and tranquility at home.

Also, in reference to the case of the wife of Thabit bin Qays, a companion of the Prophet Muhammad, when she sought divorce from her husband, she said that she did not hate him or dislike him with regard to his religion or behavior; she was just tired of him. Hence the Prophet asked Thabit to let her go as long as she returned to him the garden of dates he gave to her as a dowry. She agreed to return the dowry, and Thabit accepted it and let her go freely. Based on this, when harmonious life cannot be maintained between a husband and wife, the best solution is to depart peacefully rather than to live in an unhealthy relationship. Therefore it is my opinion in the current case that the *Shari`ah* court should have granted Habiba a divorce through *Khulu`* because she was no longer interested in living with her husband, and that was why she appealed to the *Shari`ah* court of appeal, hoping that her wish would be granted. Unfortunately she was disappointed. What happened to her when she returned to Alhaji Dahiru's house, nobody knew.

This and similar cases show that the *Shari`ah* court in Nigeria is not static. The judges are well trained and they often do their best to deliver justice, taking into consideration what is in the interests of the people. They occasionally go the extra mile to interpret the law according to the spirit of Islam rather than adhering to the letter of the law. There is great hope that in the future the situation in all *Shari`ah* courts in Nigeria will improve, especially since most of the judges who occupy the benches in the *Shari`ah* courts receive combined law degrees [Islamic law and common law] from the universities in Nigeria. As a result, they will be able to function in both civil and *Shari`ah* courts. Fortunately, not only Muslims but also Christians are studying for a degree in Islamic law.

Conclusion

Nigeria's *Shari`ah* courts adhere to the law as expressed in the Maliki school and hardly refer to other schools in their verdicts. The cases cited above are representative of the methods of application of Islamic law in Nigeria in the *Shari`ah* courts. They show that the judges are learned in Maliki law. Their decisions would have had no justification in Islamic law if they had not been interpreted as being motivated by serving the interests of the people. If the spirit of Islamic law is ruled out, these judgments would be wrong because they would not conform completely to the established rules of the classical works of Islamic law.

Moreover, married women and young girls in Nigeria occasionally turn to the courts for assistance when disputes occur between them and their husbands or parents regarding marriage. Seeking such assistance is not uncommon in the Muslim community in Nigeria. Nevertheless, the decision of any lower court is subject to revision on appeal from either party to the *Shari`ah* court of appeal. And anyone who is not satisfied with the judgment of the *Shari`ah* court of appeal can also appeal to the federal court of appeal for a final decision. The *Shari`ah* court of appeal remains under the supervision of the federal court of appeal, which has the right to endorse or review the *Shari`ah* courts' decisions.

In the first case, perhaps the decision of the lower court was endorsed and upheld by the federal court of appeal because the woman's consent is very important in Islamic marriage. Her right to choose whom to marry was given to her. The second case proved how the judges decided to grant the wife a divorce and forced the husband to pay back what he had received from her as *Khulu`*. This was a departure from the acceptable practice among the Muslims whereby a wife who seeks divorce is often requested to pay back what she received from the husband. It was motivated by the spirit of Islamic law of removing harm from the party affected. Fortunately, it has become a precedent at the *Shari`ah* courts that the wife who procures divorce will not need to pay anything back to the husband if she can prove her case. I have not found a written law or code establishing this, but through my reading of cases decided by the judges in the *Shari`ah* court of appeal in different states, I understand that this is the unwritten norm. This appears to be an attempt to practice *Ijtihad*,[77] which must be encouraged. By reviving and applying *Ijtihad* to novel issues and to legal challenges which Muslim courts face today, they would be able to establish better justice and promote peace among all members of the society. For sure, the application of Islamic law is not going away in Nigeria, so the government has to improve its procedures, and appoint qualified judges and scholars to the *Shari`ah* courts.

Amina Lawal's Case of Adultery: Free at Last

Introduction to the Case

Amina Lawal was accused of adultery and sentenced to death by stoning by the *Shari`ah* court in Katsina State, Northern Nigeria. Nigerian lawyers took up her case, defended her and finally she was set free. Her freedom was a landmark victory for the Nigerian legal system. The media and many foreign countries have criticized Nigerian secular government for allowing Islamic law to operate, particularly today. These critics forgot that Islamic law had been in operation before the arrival of the British and the introduction of foreign British common law in Nigeria.

After the inauguration of the application of Islamic law on all aspects of life in twelve states in Northern Nigeria between 2000 and 2002,[78] one of the most controversial issues in the *Shari`ah* courts was that of stoning to death for adultery, exemplified in the case of Amina Lawal in Katsina State. Amina Lawal Kurami was born in Kurami in Katsina State in 1972, in 2001 she was accused of adultery, she was found guilty at the *Shari`ah* court in Bakori, Katsina State, on March 22, 2002. She was sentenced to death by stoning. The judges claimed that their judgment was based on concrete evidence, which was her pregnancy out of wedlock.[79]

The man whom Lawal alleged to have had a relationship with her, Mallam Yahaya Muhammad, was not prosecuted because of the lack of concrete evidence to convict him. He denied having a sexual relationship with Lawal and since there were no witnesses he was set free. The conviction of Lawal and its announcement caused great uproar in Nigeria and abroad. The majority of people on hearing the news immediately accused Islam and Islamic law as barbaric, uncivilized and outdated, and which must be abandoned totally because of its alleged harshness and discrimination against women. Fortunately the human rights movement in Nigeria took up the case and teamed up with other women's organizations to create a defense team to plead for Amina Lawal's release. The outcry of many journalists and concerned people around the world was unprecedented. The case gave ample opportunity for the opponents of the application of Islamic law in Nigeria to vent their condemnation of Islam and Islamic law. They alleged that Islamic law had no foundation in the Nigerian Constitution, that the attempt to implement Islamic law was new and that Muslim judges who were entrusted with the administration of justice in these Islamic courts were not trained and therefore it was natural for them to mishandle cases. This prompted the frequent broadcast of cases of stoning to death, of cutting off hands, of lashing and of abuses of justice in the Islamic courts in the north.

Fortunately a team of lawyers got together and formed a defense team for Lawal. They insisted that the case had to be handled diligently and with caution so as not to anger the many groups that were interested in the case [if Lawal were to be free]. The defense team leader was Aliyu Musa Yawuri and not Hauwa Ibrahim, as she proudly claimed in her interviews with media groups in the USA and in Europe. Yawuri met with Amina Lawal and visited the court in Funtua in Katsina to appeal the case. The court did not grant his appeal at the beginning but later its decision was overturned. That approval gave the defense team ample opportunity to put its arguments together and to gather as much information as it could. While the defense team was working vigorously behind the scenes, the *Shari`ah* court in Funtua, the governor of Katsina and the then president of Nigeria, Olusegun Obasanjo, received thousands of letters and e-mails from home and abroad condemning the verdict of the *Shari`ah* court and accusing the country of immaturity for allowing Islamic law to be operated in a secular state like Nigeria. They required that the case against

Lawal be dismissed and her life saved from the barbaric and ancient law. President Obasanjo acted prudently and assured the citizens that he had confidence and trust in the judicial system of Nigeria, and that the court should be left alone to do its job of administering justice without pressure. He did not interfere, at least publicly. Despite all of these assurances, letters of protest continued to arrive from all over the world, especially from the USA and Europe, as if no one had ever been sentenced to death in Nigeria. Several protests were launched against Nigerian embassies around the world. People were totally outraged by the stoning sentence. These embassies assured the protests that Nigeria has three legal systems and appeal processes which would be duly followed by the defense team of Amina Lawal. Appeals go from the *Shari`ah* courts to the *Shari`ah* court of appeal, and then to the federal court of appeal in Kaduna or Lagos. Through this process, justice is guaranteed for all Nigerians.

At the first appearance of the defense team in the *Shari`ah* court on August 19, 2002, the team presented its case and arguments. The judges were not convinced and thus insisted that the stoning verdict should be carried out soon. The defense team again diligently appealed and its appeal was granted. Another date was set and the team came with its new and refined arguments, and lawyer Yawuri led the presentation in court. After a long argument and lengthy deliberation, the court adjourned. Then on September 25, 2003, the *Shari`ah* judges in a vote of four against one unanimously dismissed Amina Lawal's case and acquitted her of all accusations; she was set free. The stoning sentence was withdrawn and the case was dismissed on the basis of technical errors.[80] Lawal's life was spared: she remained the mother for her daughter, Wasila, and she remarried.

An Analysis of Amina Lawal's Case

The manner in which the *Shari`ah* court in Bakori constructed its case against Amina Lawal was questioned by the defense team. It was the state which charged Lawal with adultery after finding her pregnant when she was not married.[81] The court concluded that she was pregnant out of wedlock. She was summoned to appear in court to explain how she was pregnant. She confessed that her pregnancy was out of wedlock.[82] Based on that confession, the court charged her with adultery and sentenced her to death by stoning because she was married. She mentioned the man who had had a relationship with her, and he was summoned but later released owing to a lack of convincing evidence to charge him.

The defense team argued that the government had no right to investigate her or summon her to court because there was no eyewitness to the act of adultery, as required by the *Qur'an*. The court responded that her pregnancy was proof of her illegal relationship with another man who was not her husband. The defense team argued that punishing her alone without the man (Mallam Yahaya) with whom she conceived a baby amounted to discrimination and injustice. The man should not be freed without having his DNA tested to determine whether he was the baby's father. The court made an error here because it would have been better to conduct DNA testing before letting him go than merely to rely on his swearing on the *Qur'an* that he did not have sex with Lawal. The defense team also alleged that due process of law was not taken into consideration before Lawal was convicted of adultery (*Zina*). For instance, the team claimed that only one *Shari`ah* court judge passed the verdict on her whereas three judges should have been in attendance before announcing such a terrible verdict as stoning to death.

The *Shari`ah* court did not accept this allegation. It claimed that due process was followed and that the verdict was based on evidence collected by the court. The defense team asserted that Lawal should have been set free when she denied the allegation of adultery because in Islamic law, especially on the charges of adultery, fornication and homicide, the accused can recant their statement and thus the verdict would be reversed. The learned judges in the *Shari`ah* court did not buy into the argument because the pregnancy was strong evidence that Lawal had been involved in an illegal relationship. In addition, the argument by the defense team that considering pregnancy as evidence of a crime amounts to discrimination against women and therefore violates the principle of equality between men and women before the law was totally rejected by the *Shari`ah* court. The court argued that punishing a woman for a crime she has committed does not constitute discrimination against her. There were men who were convicted of fornication under the *Shari`ah* law in Sokoto, Bauchi, Niger, Katsina and Zamfara states and they were punished in the same way that women were punished.[83] Therefore there is no discrimination in *Zina* punishment.

When Islam applies specific rules to a specific group of people, such an application amounts to no discrimination against either male or female. For instance, in the marriage contract in Islam the man pays a dowry to the woman. No Muslim perceives this gift from the man to his wife as discrimination against the man. Aminu Adamu in his article "*Zina* (Adultery) under Islamic Law in Nigeria" has eloquently and critically refuted the idea that Islamic law's application to Amina Lawal was a bias against women as alleged by Hauwa Ibrahim, who with her other women's rights advocates have vowed to get rid of such bias in Islamic law, not only in Nigeria but all over the world. Adamu concluded his analysis of the ordeal of Amina Lawal's case by stating:

> The trial and conviction, appeal, discharge and acquittal of Amina Lawal in the charge of *Zina* under the Katsina State *Sharia* Panel Code was not gender biased.[84]

He also quoted the statement of the leading counsel in the case, Aliyu Yawuri, that Amina Lawal had nothing against the Islamic law which charged her with adultery but believed that she would find help within it and be set free:

> Amina Lawal is a Muslim; she lives in a Muslim community. She believed that the *Sharia*, under which she was convicted and sentenced to death, should contain some mechanism that could allow her appeal and set her free. In other words, she yearned for legitimacy. [And she got it and was finally set free.][85]

The case of Amina Lawal and the similar case of Safiyatu Husaini have been well documented and analyzed by Aliyu Musa Yawuri, Hauwa Ibrahim and Aminu Adamu. While many observers would assume that the acquittals of both Amina Lawal and Safiyatu Husaini were a blow and humiliation to the advocates of *Shari`ah* law's application in the north because the *Shari`ah* sentencing of both to death by stoning was finally dismissed, Yawuri, the leading counsel for both convicted women, saw their victory at the *Shari`ah* court a triumph for the *Shari`ah* and the regaining of trust in the legal system of Nigeria.[86]

In addition to the above analysis, I will also address some issues and questions raised by Hauwa Ibrahim in her article "Reflections on the Case of Amina Lawal." In her introduction, she reiterated the question of 'whether any state in Nigeria could adopt the *Shari`ah* system, whose provision prescribes more severe penalties than the penal code such as capital punishment and amputation of limbs.' Those who oppose the application of Islamic law have raised similar queries and felt that the application of Islamic capital punishment amounts to discrimination because it subjects innocent Muslims to receiving harsher punishment than other Nigerians who reside in non-*Shari`ah* states.

In response to this allegation, I affirm that the recognition and endorsement of Islamic law by the federal government and by the 1999 Constitution implies that Muslims would apply different laws, and those laws by their nature would be different from others. And if the citizens of any state agree to adopt Islamic laws which include criminal laws, they know that these laws are different from others, otherwise there would be no need for them to request the application of Islamic law. The Constitution has given each state the right to enact any law it wants as long as it is approved by the state house of assembly. That provision in the Constitution is what allows those twelve states to adopt full-scale Islamic law. In addition, it is not necessary in a federal government like that of Nigeria that every state follows the same rules of law. Each should be free to enact and adopt any law which its residents approve, just as happens in the USA. There, the state of Texas endorses capital punishment by lethal injection while many other states oppose it. The opponents of capital punishment have challenged it but whenever the government of Texas has asked its citizens to vote for or against capital punishment, the majority express support for the death penalty. As such, Texas routinely executes criminals who are on death row. The law of any particular group expresses the will of the people.

If Nigeria's northerners opted for Islamic law, and many have done so, opponents should stop accusing them of discrimination or labeling them as barbaric because they have chosen a different legal system—it is their right to choose any law they want. We should not claim that we are more concerned about them than they are concerned about themselves. English law, which we want them to adopt, was forced on Nigeria by the British during the colonial occupation. Nigerians did not choose the common law that is applied on us today. Credit should be given to the northerners who chose their own law when they had the freedom to do so. The authority of establishing laws lies in the people of the state.[87] And contrary to the alleged idea that the application of Islamic law is a recent issue in Nigeria, Islamic law is in fact the oldest written law in the country—it was there before the British occupation, and it was applied during British rule even though there were some restrictions on it. Since the independence of 1960, the *Shari`ah* has never disappeared from the country's legal system. It is not a new law there at all. In addition, the majority of cases, whether civil, family or criminal, were and are taking to the *Shari`ah* courts in across Northern Nigeria because of the trust that people have in Islamic law.

Further, the tone of Hauwa Ibrahim's articles and interviews with the media, foreign correspondents and others suggests that women are discriminated against and that they have been singled out for punishment, and therefore that the *Shari`ah* is gender biased. In response to this allegation, A. Adamu asserted that the law and penalty of *Zina* in Maliki law applies to both men and women as long as they are convicted in the court of law. He said in his article,[88]

> The penalty for *Zina* under Maliki Islamic law is not gender bias. The penalty of death by stoning falls on all persons who are either married or divorced. Once they are convicted of the crime, irrespective of gender. Unmarried convicts would ordinarily have been charged with the crime of fornication and not adultery.[89]

Adamu discussed thoroughly the allegation that Islamic law regarding adultery (*Zina*) is biased against women. He came to the conclusion that Hauwa's claim of gender bias has no foundation; that the law applied to Amina Lawal's case was not biased. He reiterated in his article:

> The trial and conviction, appeal, discharge and acquittal of Amina Lawal in the charge of *Zina* under the Katsina State *Sharia* Panel Code was not gender biased.[90]

Adamu and his legal team, after they won the case, gave reasons why Amina Lawal was finally acquitted on September 25, 2003, some of which follow:[91]

1. That, for an offense of Zina to be proved, both accused persons must be seen performing the act of Zina openly by at least four responsible male adults;
2. That discharging the man accused of being with Ms. Lawal without establishing that four witnesses had seen the act of Zina, was an error and cannot be sustained before the court;
3. That since Ms. Lawal (first accused) was not the wife of Yahaya Mohammed (the second accused) at the trial, under the Sharia Law, she cannot be charged with adultery;
4. That anyone who accuses another of Zina and cannot prove it should be flogged 40 times;
5. That where four witnesses have not been established, the accused must be discharged and acquitted;
6. That it was an abuse of the Sharia Penal Court law for a judge to sit alone at the trial when the law provided for a three judge panel;
7. That the confession of the Appellant was not valid;
8. That the trial court failed to give Ms. Lawal the opportunity to withdraw or recant her confession at least four times;

9. That where one accused person allegedly confessed and the second accused refused to confess, then that cannot be Zina;
10. That the accused person cannot swear by the Quran but can only take an oath in the name of God;
11. That the trial court record concerning Ms. Lawal's confession was unclear, and where such a doubt existed, doubt must be resolved in the favor of the accused person. The court recanted the entire story of Ma'is (a person that allegedly committed Zina) to buttress this point;
12. That the burden of proof of Zina is borne by the prosecutor and not the accused. Ms. Lawal's pregnancy and childbirth could have been the product of the former husband;
13. That an accused can withdraw a confession at any time before judgment, and the trial court must accept this; and
14. That withdrawing or recanting a confession is not punishable.

Looking at the reasons why Amina Lawal was finally acquitted, one can see some inconsistency in the court's statements. For instance, point 2 states:

> That discharging the man accused of being with Ms. Lawal without establishing that four witnesses had seen the act of Zina, was an error and cannot be sustained before the court;

First, the suspected man (Mallam Yahaya) who had an affair with Lawal was not charged. Thus his discharge was not an error. If he had been accused then there would have been a need for four witnesses. Since he was just a suspect and since the court could not prove a crime against him, he was released. It was not the discharge which was wrong as assumed but his detention in the beginning without justification.

Point 3 states:

> That since Ms. Lawal [first accused] was not the wife of Yahaya Mohammed [the second accused] at the trial, under the Sharia Law, she cannot be charged with adultery;

This statement is inaccurate. Amina Lawal did not have to be the wife of Mallam Yahaya before she could be charged with adultery. Any woman who commits adultery could be charged, whether a wife or not, but she could not be punished without concrete evidence to convict her. In Lawal's case, she confessed that she had had sex outside wedlock. If her case could be proved then she would be punished and the law would be applied to her. It is fruitless to argue that consensual sex does not constitute adultery. In Islam, any sexual relationship outside wedlock, whether the parties agreed to it or not, constitutes adultery or fornication and so is punishable by law. In this sense, since Amina Lawal became pregnant and the pregnancy was the result of sex outside wedlock, she could be charged with adultery.

In point 5 the court asserts:

> That where four witnesses have not been established, the accused must be discharged and acquitted;

This reason is inconsistent with point 2. If the defense team and the court believed in the above statement, why did the defense team accuse the court of releasing Yahaya when there were not four witnesses testifying against him? If Amina Lawal was to be released because of the absence of four witnesses to the sexual act, then Yahaya had the right to be released too. However, unfortunately, his release caused tension. Hauwa Ibrahim accused the court of acquitting him while holding Lawal responsible for *Zina*. To Hauwa Ibrahim, this release constituted discrimination against women. Yahaya should have been convicted and asked to provide DNA to establish whether he was the father of the baby carried by Lawal.

I do not agree that Lawal's confession was not valid. If she confessed to something that she did and then did not recant her confession, why should the court force her to recant it? She had ample opportunity to do so by herself but she did not. It was the defense team that suggested to her to recant her statement. However, as pointed out by Yawuri in his article,

> Ms. Lawal is a Muslim; she lives in a Muslim community. She believed that the *Sharia*, under which she was convicted and sentenced to death, should contain some mechanism that could allow her appeal and set her free.[92]

As such her confession was valid; she was pregnant, and she knew the meaning and implication of her confession. Lawal was telling the truth that could not be denied, and I think that it was that truth that led partially to her eventual acquittal and freedom.

Point 12 states:

> That the burden of proof of Zina is borne by the prosecutor and not the accused. Ms. Lawal's pregnancy and childbirth could have been the product of the former husband.

Amina Lawal knew when she was pregnant and who had had a sexual relationship with her. She did not claim that her pregnancy was from her former husband. We wonder why the court or the defense team resorted to this point when she was so sure that her pregnancy was out of wedlock. It is this type of suggestive misleading statement that keeps many Muslims skeptical about defense lawyers who occasionally twist the truth of the case to win an acquittal for their clients.

Unfortunately, since everyone was yearning for the Lawal's freedom and everyone was pleased about the dismissal of her case and her winning her freedom, no consideration was given to how she was released or the contents of the learned judges at the *Shari`ah* appeal court. While the defense team earned a lot of credit for saving their client's life, the fact remains that she committed the act of having a sexual relationship outside wedlock and this act is wrong according to Islam. Even though it was her body, in Islam one does not use one's body to disobey God's rules. Freedom lies in Islam within the parameters set by the religion. Of course, one is free to embrace Islam, but when one embraces it one is required to follow its ethical teachings. Indeed, fornication and adultery are prohibited by God. Under Islamic law, adultery is a sinful act. Amina Lawal's escape from being stoned to death was as a result of technical mismanagement of her case by the lower court and not on the basis that fornication or adultery is permissible, or that stoning is not part of Islamic law. Those twelve states which opted for the full application of Islamic law in all aspects of life, including criminal aspects, know that the law of punishment in Islam is harsh because of the seriousness of the crime, yet they voted for its application. If this is their choice, that choice should be respected. As many other Nigerians are free to follow any legal system they choose, the Muslims in the north should be free to choose their own legal system, just as the state of Texas in the USA is free to choose capital punishment despite the fact that many other states frown on it and consider it to be barbaric and inhumane. Texans pay little attention to the rhetoric of the opponents of the death penalty. They believe strongly that someone who brutally and intentionally kills an innocent person should be punished severely after conviction at the court of law.

Conclusion

Looking at the case of Amina Lawal, one can conclude that:

1. Islamic law operates in many parts of Nigeria: Sokoto, Zamfara, Katsina, Kano, Jigawa, Yobe, Bornu, Gombe, Bauchi, Kaduna, Niger and Kebbi states. Other states, such as Kogi and Kwara (in Yorubaland), also apply Islamic family law to their citizens.
2. There are due processes of the application of Islamic law, and the *Shari`ah* courts keep records of their cases.
3. The application of Islamic law in Nigeria is not new as alleged by some uninformed people. It has been in practice since the Sokoto Caliphate in 1808. When the British conquered the Sokoto Caliphate in 1903, it retained Islamic law and instituted indirect rule, in which the northern leaders were retained in their positions and their laws were practiced and endorsed by the British colonial occupier. After independence, Islamic law was in operation and it was in 1976 that the *Shari`ah* court of appeal was established to hear appeals from the lower Islamic courts.
4. The clients are free to appeal to a higher Islamic court on any judgment they receive and do not agree with. If they are not satisfied with the judgment of the *Shari`ah* court of appeal, they can appeal to the federal court of appeal in Kaduna or Lagos for a final judgment.
5. The *Shari`ah* courts allow lawyers to represent their clients. The allegation that no lawyer representation is permitted is inaccurate. Both male and female lawyers appear in the *Shari`ah* courts contrary to the claim of Hauwa Ibrahim. She was not the first lawyer to appear before the Islamic courts and not the leading defense team of Amina Lawal, as pointed out by Aliyu M. Yawuri in his article.
6. The judges at the *Shari`ah* courts receive legal training just like any other judge in the high court or appeal court in Nigeria. They also earn higher degrees in legal studies before they are appointed as judges. Even in the old northern region, the alkalis received legal education from Kano and many graduates from the Institute of Legal Studies were sent to Sudan in particular and to many other Arab countries for higher training in legal studies.
7. Islamic law (*Shari`ah*) has a key role to play in the Nigerian legal system. There is no genuine reason to presume its abandonment in

the near future. Rather, it may be extended to other states (e.g. Lagos, Oyo and Osun states) which have not yet accepted it.

I shall conclude this chapter with a quote from Yawuri, the leader of Amina Lawal's defense team:

> I personally hold the opinion that despite the human deficiencies in the implementation of *Sharia, the Sharia has brought a lot of positive changes in the society.* But it is being implemented under the circumstances of mistrust that I have mentioned. It behooves a responsible counsel involved in the application of the laws and the correction of errors in their application to circumspect. It is in the view of this that the [Women's Rights Advancement and Protection Alternative] resolved not to sensationalize these two cases [of Safiyatu Husaini and Amina Lawal]. Every day, all over Nigeria, thousands of lawyers, women and men, Muslims and Christians, working for government agencies, [non-governmental organizations] and private law firms, under very difficult conditions, are doing their quiet best to make the legal systems of the Federation and of the States work the way they are supposed to work, and they are often succeeding. They do not occupy the media and international limelight, but they are the true heroes of the fight for the rule of law in Nigeria.[93]

Truly they are the heroes and they deserve respect from all Nigerians.

NOTES

1. Justice Kui Ya Alkali, "The Area Courts in Kano State" (paper presented at the 1989 Law Week at Faculty of law, Bayero University, Kano, May 31, 1989), pp. 1–3.
2. Ya Alkali, pp. 3–4.
3. There are few cases where the lawyers are not allowed but, today, lawyers represent their clients at the *Shari`ah* courts, especially in Kwara State and many of the northern states, as seen in Amina Lawal's and Safiyatu Husaini's cases. Both were represented by a team of lawyers headed by Aliyu M. Yawuri.
4. Customary laws are the unwritten ethnic laws that apply to a particular group of people. They are accepted by members of a community as binding among them. They vary from one ethnic group to another. In Nigeria, customary law is the indigenous law which is neither Islamic nor English. For more information about customary laws in Nigeria, see A. O. Obilade, *The Nigerian Legal System* (London: Sweet & Maxwell, 1979), pp. 83–110.

5. Ya Alkali, p. 4.
6. Musa Ali Ajetunmobi, "*Shari`ah* Legal Practice in Nigeria 1956–1983" (PhD diss., University of Ilorin, Department of Islamic Studies, June 1988), p. 71.
7. Ajetunmobi, p. 76.
8. Ya Alkali, pp. 11–12.
9. Ya Alkali, p. 12.
10. Ya Alkali, pp. 13–15.
11. S. K. Rashid, ed. *Islamic Law in Nigeria* (Lagos: Islamic Publication Bureau, 1986), pp. 242–243.
12. Obilade, pp. 183–184.
13. The *Shari`ah Court of Appeal Law* (N. N. Laws 1963).
14. The Constitution of the Federation of Nigeria as amended by the Constitution Assembly 2, decree 1976. See Obilade, pp. 176–177.
15. Ishaq O. Oloyede, "*Mukhtasar Khalil* and the Understanding of Islamic law in Nigeria." *Hamdard Islamicus* 12, no. 1 (1987): 83–90.
16. However, Islam seeks the support and endorsement of the bride's father to safeguard her interests. The final consent rests with the bride.
17. For more information about the decline of the rights of women in the medieval age, see Lamya al-Faruqi, *Women, Muslims, and Islam* (Indianapolis: American Trust Publication, 1988). The author details the history of women's rights from the time of the Prophet Muhammad up to the present.
18. For more information about the status of women in Islam, see Lamya' Al-Faruqi, *Women, Muslim Society and Islam* (Indianapolis: American Trust Publication, 1988), pp. 63–76.
19. There are a few cases nowadays addressed by Hauwa Ibrahim which she took over by herself in her support for women rights, especially after the establishment of the total application of Islamic law in twelve northern states after 1999. She was a member of the defense team for Amina Lawal but not the leading lawyer, as she claimed.
20. I partly discussed this case in one of my other articles on the application of Islamic law in Nigeria in *Journal of Islamic Studies*, Pakistan, 1992.
21. The reason why the father turned down one of the suitors was not explained in the reports that I read, but it was probably because he was not as rich or famous as the other suitor.
22. For convenience, I use the first names of the appellants and defendants.
23. The reason why Karimatu's father preferred Alhaji Umaru to marry his daughter was not mentioned in the documents I read. He might have been considering some qualities of Alhaji Umaru which I am unaware of.
24. One may speculate that Karimatu's father insisted that she marry Alhaji Umaru because he had sent gifts and messages to him. People had known that he was proposing to marry Karimatu. It is unusual for a father-in-law to say no after he had said yes.

25. For more details about the letters she wrote to her uncle and her reasons for taking such steps, see Ajetunmobi's PhD dissertation, pp. 529–535.
26. Alhaji Ma'aji Isa Shani and Mohammad Altaf Hussain Ahangar, "Marriage Guardianship in Islam: Reflections on a Recent Nigerian Judgment," *Islamic and Comparative Law Quarterly* 6, no. 4 (1986): 278. The only reason given by the area court in making its judgment is the lack of consent from the girl, which constitutes the backbone of a marriage contract, and the first condition to be met in all Islamic marriages; this is known as 'offer and acceptance' (*ijab wa qabul*) in Islamic law.
27. That the second marriage was conducted between Karimatu and Alhaji Mahmoud apparently showed that she was interested in marriage.
28. F. H. Ruxton, *Maliki Law* (Connecticut: Hyperion Press Inc., Westport, 1980), p. 92. One wonders how the judges in the *Shari`ah* Court of Appeal endorsed such a decision despite much evidence to the contrary in the *Hadith* of the Prophet.
29. The *iddah* (waiting or mourning period) is the interval of time that a woman must wait after divorce or the death of her husband before she can remarry. Glasse, p. 179.
30. Ajetunmobi, p. 532.
31. The latter reason is suggested for the area court's decision.
32. Alhaji Isa Shani and Ahangar's article (p. 278) quoting Charles Hamilton, *The Hedaya or Guide: A Commentary on the Mussulman Laws* (India, Delhi: Islamic Book Trust, 1982), pp. 34–36. See also Shaykh Muhammad 'Arafah al-Dasuki, *Hashiyat al-Dasuki 'Ala Al-Sharh al-Kabir* (Cairo: Isa al-Babi al-Halabi wa Sharkah, 1980), 2:222–23; Wahbah al-Zuhayli, *al-Fiqh al-Islami wa Adilatuhu* (Beirut: Dar al-Fikr, 1986), 7:201. The reason for assigning this power to the father is either that the daughter has no experience about family life or because she is still a virgin. Not all Maliki scholars subscribe to this view.
33. Both Alhaji Paiko and Alhaji Mahmud were represented by lawyers at the federal court of appeal.
34. Ajetunmobi, p. 546; al-Dasuki, 2:223; al-Zuhayli, *al-Fiqh al-Islami*, 7:201.
35. The *Hadith* is what the Prophet Muhammad said, did and approved. At times it is used losely to include the normative traditions of Muhammad and his companions.
36. Muhammad bin Ali bin Muhammad al-Shawkani, *Nayl al-Awtar Sharh Muntaqa al-Akhbar min Ahadith Sayyid al-Anam* (Cairo: Matba'at Mustafa al-Babi al-Halabi, 1961), 6:137.
37. Al-Shawkani, 6:138.
38. Abu al-Barakat Ahmad ibn Muhammad ibn Ahmad al-Dirdir, *Al-Sharh al-Saghir 'ala Aqrab al-Masalik ila Madhhab al-Imam Maliki* (Cairo: Dar

al-Ma'arif, 1972), vol. 2, pp. 372–373. See also Sayyid Sabiq, *Fiqh al-Sunnah* (Beirut: Dar al-Kitab al-Arabi, 1969), vol. 2, pp. 34–38.

39. Imam Malik ibn Anas, *Muwatta 'Malik* (Beirut: Mu'asasat Dar al-Tahrir li tiba'ah wa al-Nashr, 1967), p. 231.
40. Imam Malik, *al-Muwatta'*, p. 232. Such marriages were occasionally revoked when the women objected to them, as in the case of a lady who came to the Prophet complaining that her father married her to someone she did not like. The Prophet gave her a choice but she remained with the husband and she commented that she wanted other women to know that they have the right to say no to what they did not like. Al-Shawkani, 6:137–38.
41. Abu al-Walid Ahmad Muhammad ibn Rushd al-Hafid, *Bidayat al-Mujtahid wa Nihayat al-Muqtasid* (Cairo: Matba'at Mustafa al-Babi al-Halabi, 1960), vol. 2, pp. 4–5; Al-Dirdir, 2:372; Al-Zuhayli, *al-Fiqh al-Islami*, 7:78.
42. Al-Shawkani, 6:137–38. The majority of the Muslim scholars objected to the opinion of Ibn Hazm in this case because a minor has no right to make a decision about her marriage.
43. Al-Shawkani, 6:140.
44. Al-Shawkani, 6:138.
45. Al-Dirdir, 2:372. Al-Dirdir emphasizes that no party should be forced into a marriage. To him, when force is used, the marriage is void.
46. Sahnun was a Maliki jurist who recorded *al-Mudawwanah al-Kubra* from Ibn al-Qasim.
47. Imam Malik ibn Anas, *Al-Mudawwanah al-Kubra* (Cairo: al-Matba`at al-Khayriyyah, 1963), vol. 2, p. 155.
48. It is ironic that some Muslim scholars often insist that Muslim woman must marry. This is not necessary in Islam. Even though Islam encourages marriage, it does not make it compulsory. Men and women are free to marry or not marry if they choose. If they choose not to marry they should be left alone as long as they do not commit fornication.
49. Imam Malik, *al-Mudawwanah*, 2:155.
50. Yahya ibn Sharaf al-Din al-Nawawi, *Sahih Muslim bi Sharh al-Nawawi* (Cairo: al-Matba'at al-Misriyyah, 1960), vol. 9, p. 205.
51. The reason is that her father wanted her to marry Alhaji Mahmud, and then she was interested in Alhaji Umaru. However, when she changed her mind and preferred to marry Alhaji Mahmud, her father objected, probably because he would be considered weak person as a result of his inability to enforce his opinion on his daughter.
52. Al-Nawawi, 9:205.
53. Al-Qastalani Shihab al-Din Ahmad ibn Muhammad, *Irshad al-Sari: Sharh Sahih al-Bukhari* (Beirut: Dar Sadir, n.d.), vol. 8, p. 55.

54. Sayyid Sabiq, Fiqh al-*Sunnah* (Beirut: Dar al-Kitab al-Arabi, 1969), vol. 2, p. 131. The Maliki's definition of *bikr* is one who has never had sexual relations with the opposite sex following puberty, whether she is young or old.
55. Imam Malik, *al-Mudawwanah*, 2:155–58.
56. Umar Abdullah, "Malik's Concept of 'Amal' in the Light of Maliki Legal Theory" (PhD diss., University of Chicago, 1978), 1:144.
57. Case # SCA/NWS/SV/47/70 of March 19, 1971.
58. Al-Dasuki, 2:223.
59. In this case the *Shari`ah* court of appeal has accused the judges at the area court of making *ijtihad*, which it has no right to make. What qualifies the judges at the *Shari`ah* court of appeal to make *ijtihad* and excludes the judges at the area court? In my opinion there is no difference between the judges in these courts because those in the area courts are often promoted to the *Shari`ah* court of appeal.
60. For example, divorce can be procured when both cannot live together peacefully, or when one party cannot discharge their duty as husband or wife. Muslims claim that there are genuine justifications for divorce. However, not all justifications are valid. At the same time, it would be naive to assume that a wife has no right to divorce. For more information about divorce and its justification, see Hammudah 'Abd al-Ati, *Family Structure in Islam* (Indianapolis: American Trust Publications, 1977), pp. 217–228.
61. This assertion is based on a number of cases I collected during my fieldwork in Nigeria in 1989, 2004 and 2007. The husbands misused their right and thus divorced their wives because the latter asked them to support them financially.
62. *Qur'an* 2:229–32.
63. Ibn Rushd, 2:66–70; see also al-Shawkani, 6:278. One of the scholars who objected to this form of marriage was Bakr ibn 'Abd Allah al-Muzani, see al-Shawkani, 2:278.
64. Ibn Rushd, 2:98; al-Zuhayli, *al-Fiqh al-Islami*, 7: 527.
65. Muhammad ibn Idris al-Shafi'i, *Al-Umm* (Beirut: Dar al-Ma'rifah, 1973), vol. 5, p. 177; al-Zuhayli, *al-Fiqh al-Islami*, 7:527; al-Muti'i, 15:609.
66. *Hasan Gbaguda v. Muhammad Gbaguda*. Case # SCA/NS/CV/161/1980 of October 31, 1980.
67. The beating was established, in addition to his confession, through the hospital bills which Hasana brought to the court. She was admitted to hospital because of the physical injuries that she received from the beating.
68. To return to him the amount she received from him as a dowry.
69. One may wonder why she couldn't leave. The answer is that if she left without being legally separated, she would not be able to find another

husband. The society is totally interconnected. People do not marry without a thorough investigation of their potential spouse's background, especially in the case of a divorcee or a widow.

70. In my view, a reference should have been made to a *hadith* where the Prophet Muhammad advised Thabit's wife to seek *Khulu*` when her husband broke her hand during fighting. The Prophet asked Thabit to take whatever he gave her as a dowry and then let her go. He agreed and she divorced him. See al-Shawkani, 6:676–77.
71. It must be emphasized that divorce is a conventional thing. Everyone is free to marry or not to marry. However, after marriage the right to divorce is conventional. That is, each community agrees on how it should be carried out.
72. See the *hadith* reported by Ibn Abbas in which he said that Jamilah bint Salul came to the Prophet complaining about her husband. The Prophet told her to return to her husband what she had received from him. See Ibn Rushd, 2:66–70; al-Shawkani, 6:276–77.
73. *Al-Fawakih al-Dawani matn al-Nafarawi*, p. 86, quoted from the case record p. 2. This is a book written in the Hausa language. The case record does not give the source of this book or the author's name.
74. Al-Shawkani, 6:277. In the *hadith* about Thabit's wife, the Prophet's judgment was that she should return what she received from Thabit if she really wanted a divorce.
75. Dasuki, *Mukhtasar al-Khalil,* vol. 2, p. 319.
76. *Juwahir Iklil*, a commentary on *Mukhtasar*, ch 1 p. 336.
77. *Ijtihad* is the exercising or giving of independent judgment concerning matters pertaining to the religious sciences and more specifically Islamic law on the part of those who are learned in Islam law. See H. Nasr, *Islam, Ideals, and Realities* (Boston: Beacon Press, 1972), p. 180. It is also defined as the logical deduction regarding a legal or theological question by a learned and enlightened doctor (*Mujtahid*). See Highest, p. 197. Often, *Ijtihad* applies to those questions which are not covered by the *Qur'an* or the *Sunnah* of the Prophet Muhammad.
78. These states are Sokoto, Zamfara, Katsina, Kano, Jigawa, Yobe, Bornu, Gombe, Bauchi, Kaduna, Niger and Kebbi. In the southern part of Nigeria, both Kwara and Kogi apply Islamic law in family issues.
79. The sentence of stoning an adulterer to death was not mentioned in the *Qur'an*. However, there are several cases of stoning to death in the *Hadith* and in the practice of the immediate followers of the Prophet Muhammad. To Muslims, both the *Qur'an* and the *Hadith* are authentic primary sources of Islamic law. The argument that stoning is unlawful because of its absence from the *Qur'an* has no merit. Many rules in Islam are not derived directly from the *Qur'an* but from the *Hadith*. The rejection of any law on

the grounds that it is not mentioned in the *Qur'an* is tantamount to rejecting the *Qur'an* itself. Therefore Muslim scholars agree that there is stoning in Islam and that it was practiced when Prophet Muhammad was alive. Whether stoning should be practiced today is an entirely new question which Muslim scholars should address critically. It should be viewed in the same way that Muslim scholars view slavery today. No one advocates slavery today, so by the same token we should re-evaluate the issue of stoning and rethink its application. Its practice does harm to Muslims, tarnishes their image and generates hate against them.

80. The appeal court dismissed the case on the grounds that the lower court made mistakes in the process, thus Amina Lawal was set free. So far no one has been stoned to death in Nigeria since the 2000 inauguration of Islamic law in Nigeria.
81. *Amina Lawal v. The State* (KTS/SCA/FT/86/2002), supra note 6.
82. It was reported that she had an affair with Mallam Yahaya Muhammad for eleven months prior to her charge in court on January 15, 2002. That relationship ended in Lawal's pregnancy. She finally had a baby named Wasila. When Mallam Yahaya Muhammad was charged, he argued that he did not have a sexual relationship with her. Since there was insufficient evidence to convict him, he was released. His release was considered by feminists to represent discrimination against woman. The feminists argue that if Amina Lawal were to be punished, Mallam Muhammad should be punished too. At least he should have not been released without a DNA test to ascertain whether or not he was the father of the baby. If he was he should be convicted too. See Aminu Adamu's article, "Zina (Adultery) Under Islamic Law in Nigeria," in SSRN-abstract 1119684, Social Science Research Network, April 16, 2008, accessed on June 20, 2015.
83. Mark Duff, "Nigerian Man Faces Death for Adultery," *BBC News*, June 27, 2002. Http://news.bbc.co.uk/1/hi/world/Africa/2070594.htm
84. Aminu Adamu, "Zina (Adultery) Under Islamic Law in Nigeria."
85. Aliyu Musa Yawuri, "On Defending Safiyatu Husaini and Amina Lawal" in Philip Ostein et al. (eds), *Shari`ah Implementation in Northern Nigeria 1999–2006: A Source Book*, vol. 5, p. 133.
86. Yawuri, p. 139.
87. See Aminu Adamu Bello's "Zina (Adultery) under Islamic Law." The Shari`ah was not forced on the people in the north; they chose it.
88. Ibid, p. 9; see also *Qur'an* ch 24:2 (surat al-Nur).
89. Ibid, p. 19.
90. Ibid, p. 19.
91. Ibrahim, Hauwa. "Rule of Law Prevails in the Case of Amina Lawal." *Human Rights Brief* 11, no. 3 (2004): 39–41.

92. Aliyu Musa Yawuri, "On Defending Safiyatu Husaini and Amina Lawal," p. 133.
93. Aliyu Musa Yawuri, "On Defending Safiyatu Husaini and Amina Lawal,' in *Shari`ah Implementation in Northern Nigeria 1999–2006: A Source Book,* vol. V, p. 139.

CHAPTER 5

Christians' Response to the Application of Islamic Law in Nigeria

Introduction

Islam since its inception has had a strong relationship with Christianity and Christians. It is one of the world religions which recognizes both Christianity and Judaism as revealed religions, and their followers are called 'people of the book' (*ahl al-Kitab*). Many Christians, even today, are unaware that Muslims have a knowledge of Christianity. They are often astonished when informed that the *Qur'an* accords great respect to biblical prophets such as Moses, Jacob, Abraham, Solomon, David and Jesus. The *Qur'an* actually devotes a whole chapter to Mary. Jesus' name appears in the *Qur'an* twenty-five times as "Isa" and eleven times as "messiah." Muhammad, the prophet of Islam, from the beginning, respected Christianity and Judaism. The revelation he received from God, known as the *Qur'an*, detailed their stories. The relationship between Islam and Christianity began immediately Muhammad received his first revelation from God on Mount Hira in Mecca in 610 CE. When the angel Gabriel spoke to Muhammad for the first time, he was frightened and ran home to his wife, Khadijah, who comforted him and assured him of her support. Seeing that Muhammad was not fully satisfied with her response, Khadijah took him to her cousin, *Waraqat bin Nawfal*, who was described in Muslim literature as *Hanif* (a puritan or one who is upright). *Waraqah* had the knowledge of the scripture, the Bible.

Waraqah, after listening carefully to what Muhammad told him about his experience on Mount Hira, said that if he was telling the truth, he

Y. Sodiq, *A History of the Application of Islamic Law in Nigeria*,
DOI 10.1007/978-3-319-50600-5_5

would be the awaited messiah for the Arabs. He added that the message that he had received was similar to that received by Moses and Jesus. He assured him of his support for as long as he was alive. He prophesized that the Quraysh would reject Muhammad, denounce his message and exile him. Muhammad was astonished to hear this. *Waraqah* told him that no prophet had come to his people with truth without being rejected and humiliated. That conversation marked the beginning of the relationship between Muslims and Christians.

Eventually, Muhammad began preaching his message in Mecca. A few accepted it and embraced Islam, while the majority opposed him and rejected his call. The Quraysh, his tribe, feared that his message would be a threat to their religious, political and economic systems. When they failed to stop Muhammad through persuasion and bargaining, they resorted to violence and persecution of him and his followers. After a few years, the persecution reached an unbearable level and the enmity grew intense. Thus Muhammad gave permission to his followers to seek refuge in another city. They were exiled to Abyssinia in Ethiopia where they were warmly received by Negus, the Christian King. That was the first migration in Islam and the first time the Muslims as a minority lived in a majority Christian environment. The Muslims stayed in Ethiopia peacefully; some spent a few months before returning to Mecca; others spent several years and even died there. It was a great experience for both Muslims and Christians.[1]

Despite the fact that Muhammad respected Christians and sought their help whenever he needed it in his early life, many Jews and Christians in the medieval age, including some prominent leaders and theologians of these religions, such as Martin Luther and Thomas Aquinas, gave little respect to Muhammad and Islam even though they read about him. They felt obligated at times to undermine him to prove their superiority over Islam and its prophet, because they saw Islam is a rival to Christianity and Judaism. This attitude stems from inadequate knowledge and a misunderstanding of Islam and of the *Qur'an*. The competition to win followers may be responsible for this strained relationship between Islam and Christianity in the medieval age. Both religions are exclusive traditions; they both struggle to win the hearts of those they presumably think of as unbelievers (gentiles, lost sheep and *Kuffar*), who need to be saved. Muslims and Christians strongly believe in the universality of their religions; both claim to have the monopoly of the truth (exclusive concept). Some Christians claim that anyone who does not believe in Jesus as the Savior will not be saved regardless of however hard he works. Salvation,

Christians argue, is a gift, and it can only be attained through faith in Jesus. Saint Cyprian (d. 258) argues that nothing less than full membership of the Catholic Church would avail a heretic of salvation, not even the baptism of blood. He then quotes Jesus' words in Matthew 12:30: "He who is not with me is against me, and he who does not gather with me scatters."[2] Also the participants at the Council of Florence (1438–1445) reiterated the same doctrine in which only Christians will be saved.

The Holy Roman Church believes, professes and preaches that no one remaining outside the Catholic Church, not just pagans but also Jews, heretics and schismatics, can partake of eternal life; instead they will go to the everlasting fire, which was prepared for the devil and his angels, unless before the end of life they are joined to the Church.[3]

Regardless of the above perceptions and polemic writings against Islam, Bernard Lewis, a Christian Islamic scholar, eloquently describes the relationship between Muslims and Christians in the medieval age as follows:

> The Europeans (Christians and Jews) and the Muslims, in contrast, knew—or thought they knew—a great deal about each other. *They had been neighbors since the very beginnings of Islam in the seventh century—neighbors in constant contact and communication, often as rivals, sometimes as enemies, and with attitudes toward each other formed and confirmed by centuries of experience and, for the Europeans, of fear* … Europe and Islam were old acquaintances, intimate enemies, whose continuing conflict derived a special virulence from their shared origins and common aims.[4]

From the above one can conclude that both Islam and Christianity are revealed religions and adherents of both traditions have lived, and continue to live, together in different parts of the world harmoniously. They are unavoidable neighbors.[5]

Christian Responses to the Application of Islamic Law in Nigeria

Nigeria remains a homeland for both Islam and Christianity; both religions are indigenous to the country. Nigeria harbors the largest Muslim and Christian population in Africa. Muslims and Christians have lived together peacefully for decades there.[6] Of course, Islam existed in Nigeria for centuries before the arrival of Christianity. When Christianity came under the tutelage of the British Empire, Muslims in Yorubaland received them warmly until Christians gradually began to establish themselves. Tension eventually emerged when the Christians, under pressure from foreign missionaries and relentless efforts of modernization, deliberately began to crush Islam and despise Muslims through Western education, which was spread by Christian missionaries.[7] These foreign missionaries were the tools of the British Empire wherever they went.[8]

The British took over Nigeria, finally conquering the Sokoto Caliphate in the north in 1903 and trying to impose its laws over Nigeria by force. Since Christians then had just begun to exist, they had nothing to object to in terms of law. The southern Yoruba and Ibo had no written laws to challenge the British imposed laws and they were happy that the British were introducing new ones. On the other hand, the northerners had existing and well-established Islamic laws and thus objected to British law. In reality, Christians have no criminal law; they always follow the law of the land in which they reside. What was known to be Christian law was Jewish law or British or European laws. Hence the Christians have little to defend as far as the law is concerned. Perhaps there are moral injunctions in the New Testament but no laws as we understand them today. If a Christian kills someone, or steals or slanders, how would they be judged according to the New Testament? The victim or their family would be encouraged to forgive the offender. This is not law in the real sense of the word but instead a set of moral values. The civil society relies on the legal system to maintain peace and order in the society. A law is a rule whose commission or violation is backed up by punishment or reward. A law holds individuals responsible for their actions, establishes justice and restores God's natural order.[9] A law could be a divine law such as Islamic law or the Ten Commandments, or manmade law like common law in European countries and the USA.

When the British conquered the northerners they promised not to tamper with the existing Islamic law but gradually began to modify it to conform to Western law. The Muslims strongly objected to the British attempt to curb Islamic law. That objection continued until the departure of the British and the independence of Nigeria in 1960. Muslims in the north were waiting for the day when they would be able to return to the full application of Islamic law to regain their lost legal rights. Indeed, the demand for the full application of Islamic law never ceased until 1999 when Zamfara State opted for its full application. Consequently, twelve other northern states followed suit and their citizens demanded the full application of Islamic law, and they won. The Muslim north perceives the reintroduction of the *Shari`ah* as the restitution of their rights and glory, which they claimed they lost during colonial rule, as pointed out by Frieder Ludwig in his article.[10] This reintroduction of the *Shari`ah* created havoc in the country, especially among Christians, who considered such a return to the full application of Islamic law as "a step toward Islamization of Nigeria."[11] It nearly caused the division of the country into two in the north and the south.[12] The following analysis details Christian responses to the application of Islamic law.

There are three major responses or approaches to this application:

1. Responses from intellectual aspects, expressing arguments against Islamic law application. These are provided by Christian scholars from different region, and they are well structured and well articulated.
2. Responses from theological perspectives, expressing the rejection of Islam as a legitimate religion, which is seen as evil by its nature (as projected by Christian fundamentalists), thus its laws are evil too. These are Islamophobia in disguise—the fear of anything Islamic without reasonable justification.
3. Responses from political and social perspectives. These are represented by those who view the application of Islamic law as politically motivated and a tool of domination and oppression. These groups perceive Islam as a rival to Christianity and thus they want to make sure that it does not progress. They believe that whatever Nigerian Muslims receive materially or politically, they should earn the same since they are all Nigerians. Islam should not be used to deprive them of their share of the "legitimate national cake."

Responses from Intellectual Perspectives

Christian scholars who argue against the application of Islamic law claim that Muslims want Islamic law to be the law of the land instead of the 1999 Constitution. They think that Muslims perceive the Constitution as 'godless law' derived from the British pagan Roman law, and since they are Muslims they do not want to be governed by it.[13] Joseph Kenny, the author of "Sharia and Christianity in Nigeria," cites a speech by Malaam Ma'aji Shani at Minna Seminar (Niger State) who calls for the *Shari`ah* to be the law of Nigeria in place of the Constitution.[14]

This assertion has no strong foundation. The proponents of Islamic law admit that the Constitution has supremacy over Islamic law and that the final appeal in any legal controversy is referred to the federal courts of appeal; this demonstrates that the Nigerian constitution is supreme. The *Shari`ah* courts remain under the supervision of the federal courts of appeal. Hence the *Shari`ah* has no supremacy over the Constitution. In fact, there are federal high courts in every state and citizens are free to take their cases to these courts rather than to the *Shari`ah* courts.

Another objection is the claim of Muslims that Islamic law would not be applied to Christians. Kenny considers such a promise made by Muslims to be unrealistic. He argues that anyone who is acquainted with the *Shari`ah* knows that Christians are treated as *Dhimmi* (protected second-class citizens). He questions why Nigerian Christians should be treated as such in their own country. Such degradation is tantamount to unfair treatment. Therefore Christians are requesting that Nigerian "secular law" be applied to all citizens regardless of their faith, without discrimination,[15] and that the *Shari`ah* be banned.

The proponents of Islamic law offer no convincing response to this challenge, except for saying that the Christians are free to apply their own laws if they so desire. And since Nigerian Christians have no specific well-structured laws of their own, they could not realistically ask the government for any application of Christian law.[16] Indeed, the Nigerian legal system recognizes various laws: English law, Native law and Islamic law. If Christians want Christian law, it could be granted. However, Ludwig, Frieder points out in his article that each state which applies the *Shari`ah* has its own unique features in that each state applies Islamic law differently and proportionately according to the needs of its citizens and constituencies, as seen in Kaduna, Katsina and Gombe states. These three states have a large number of Christians so they do not fully apply Islamic law on non-Muslims.[17] The interests of all citizens of those states are respected and safeguarded. They live with one another peacefully and work together to prevent any tension among them. Social and economic benefits are distributed fairly and equitably. Muslims in those states take their cases to the Shari`ah courts, while Christians take their cases to magistrates' courts or the state high court (which is an English court).

Unfortunately, English law overrides other laws in Nigeria despite the fact that it is a foreign law imposed by the colonial regime. On the issue of *Dhimmi* (protected citizens), it is true that Islam adopts such a rule against the people of the book: the Jews and Christians on territories that are conquered by a Muslim army in battle. Since Nigeria is not in a territory conquered by Muslims, there is no justification to apply *Dhimmi* on the country's citizens. Therefore the proponents of Islamic law argue that Christians' fear of *Dhimmi* is unjustified. Muslims and Christians are neighbors in Nigeria and they have lived together peacefully for decades. It is time for both religions to recognize that they have to relate to one another, and no one group would cease to exist because of the other because they are all Nigerian citizens. That *Dhimmi* is in an Islamic book does not mean that it should be applied to Nigerian Christians.

Another response to the application of Islamic law was the allegation of funding and financing the *Shari`ah* courts by both the state and federal governments. Such funding constitutes unfair distribution of Nigerian wealth whereby one party (Nigerian Muslims) benefits more than others in a very subtle way despite the fact that this wealth belongs to all Nigerians—Muslims and non-Muslims. This allegation is put forward by the Christian Association of Nigeria (CAN).[18]

The proponents of Islamic law respond that such a criticism has no foundation because both the state and federal governments have an obligation to finance legal institutions of the country regardless of how they came into existence because those legal institutions serve the needs of Nigerian citizens. Even though the majority of Muslims to whom the *Shari`ah* is applied go to the *Shari`ah* courts, non-Muslims also go to the *Shari`ah* courts when they choose to. The government should be responsible for the distribution of justice all over Nigeria regardless of whether the inhabitants are Muslims or non-Muslims. Also, there are courts in Eastern and Southern Nigeria whose citizens are Christians, yet both federal and state governments sponsor and fund them. If such funding and sponsorship can be offered to the people of Southern and Eastern Nigeria, why should the Muslims in the north be deprived of it? The government builds courts and pays wages to the employees in those courts in the south as well as for Muslim judges in the north. Thus there exists no discrimination or privileging of northerners over southerners. It is a required duty of the government to adjudicate and fund legal institutions, whether they are Islamic or non- Islamic. In addition, each state has high and magistrates' courts which are English courts; both Muslims and non-Muslims take their cases to these courts as they wish. All are funded by both the federal and the state governments.

Responses from Christian Evangelicals and Pentecostal Leaders

This group attempts to denounce Islam from its root, alleging that Islam amounts to evil religion and that Muslims are worshipping an "idol" known as "Allah." Thus Muslims are not true believers but pagans and devil people. It also argues that "Islam is a religion of Adam," as claimed by the Prophet Muhammad, thus it is a religion created by human beings rather than by God and so it amounts to a religion of sin, which drove human beings out of paradise. Jesus, this group argues, came to save humans from the original sin committed by Adam. Islam, on the other hand, wants to perpetuate the religion of sin by not believing in Jesus and taking people away from true salvation. This group wonders why someone should follow Islam and worship Allah, one of the gods of Mecca. Hence if Islam can be dismissed as an illegitimate religion, then its laws can be dismissed too.[19] Unfortunately, the Evangelists and Pentecostals continue to repeat this allegation, which lacks concrete and convincing evidence. Whatever bad names today's Evangelicals and Pentecostal groups may call Muhammad, the people of Mecca (the Quraysh—Muhammad's tribe) called him the same names previously. He ignored them and continued with his preaching. Within a few decades, Islam spread all over the Arabian Peninsula, and within half a century, Muslims had conquered the Roman and Byzantine empires. By 711 CE, Islam had reached Spain, and it stayed there for more than 700 years. Islam is one of the largest religions in the world and cannot be brushed off as evil. It recognizes Jesus as one of the greatest prophets but not as "God incarnated." Muslims believe that the true God cannot be crucified by human beings for God is all-powerful. Indeed, there is nothing good which Christianity offers to humanity which Islam does not offer to its adherents, including a good spiritual life, salvation and eternal life in the next life. To believe that Islam is a religion of evil is Islamophobic. Muslims and Christians have lived together in all parts of the world, and "a tradition of peaceful coexistence is available between Muslims and Christians in Nigeria."[20] Akinade even mentions in his work that early Christian missionaries in Nigeria, particularly in Yorubaland, were impressed by the Muslim attitudes toward life and toward their Christian converts. They welcomed them, and socialized and lived together with them.[21]

In addition, "Allah" is an Arabic name for God. Hence both Arab Christians and Arab Jews call God "Allah" in Arabia. On the other hand, the allegation that Adam sinned has nothing to do with the application of Islamic law. Whether a Nigerian believes in Adam as a sinner or not has no relevance to the application of the law. Justice must be applied to both Muslims and non-Muslims. Muslim scholars continuously question the idea of the original sin in Christianity. They argue that if Adam committed a sin thousands of years ago, why should Christians today in Nigeria be responsible for it, particularly when the Bible asserts that the son would not suffer or be responsible for the sins of his father?[22] If Jesus took away all human sin through his sacrifice, why should any Christian today be worried again or be responsible for it? Also, drawing on Christian reasoning, if Adam did not sin, there would not be a need for the existence and coming of Jesus. Therefore Christians should be happy that Adam committed a sin and thus gave Jesus reason to come to earth to rescue them. No one would truly know the value and commitment of Jesus if not for Adam's sin.[23] Islam is not a religion of sin but a belief in the oneness of God.

In conclusion, the idea that Islam is a devil religion and that Muhammad worshipped an idol is an old story that has been told over and over by the opponents of Islam, especially by Christian fundamentalists and the orientalists.[24] Islam is a monotheistic religion which preaches the unity of God. The Evangelists and Pentecostal leaders who perpetuate negative ideas about Islam should learn more about the religion and its doctrine of the unity of God (*Tawheed*).[25]

Christian Response from Political and Social Perspectives

The CAN and some Christian Evangelicals argue that:

1. Granting permission to Muslims to apply Islamic law amounts to giving them privileges which will allow them to propagate Islam and use public land freely for building their institutions. Other benefits include scholarships to perform pilgrimage to Mecca (*Hajj*) and paying the salaries of imams (Muslim leaders).
2. The fact of the *Shari`ah* becoming the law in some states boosts Muslim morale and lets them feel superior to other Nigerian citizens.
3. The government grants funds to Muslims to build their mosques while denying Christians permission to build new churches. When Christians are occasionally granted land, the northern Muslims won't allow them to use them, or destroy them after they have been built,[26] and the government failed to bring those responsible for the destruction to justice. Thus the CAN demanded the following to remedy the above injustices and unfair treatment of Christians:
   a. The government should sponsor Christians on pilgrimage to Rome or Jerusalem (a visit which is not religiously required by Christianity). Thus President Goodluck, Jonathan's visit to Israel in 2013 was heralded as a pilgrimage to the Holy Land and not just a diplomatic visit.

b. The Church leaders and dispute mediators should be paid a salary just like the imams and Muslim judges in the *Shari`ah* courts.
c. The federal government should restore its political relationship with the State of Israel, which was cut off in 1973 and remains strained.
d. Christians should be allowed to buy land and acquire property to build their churches wherever they want in the north.
e. Christian courts and mediation centers should be set up and funded by the federal government, just as it did for the Muslims through the establishment of Islamic courts.
f. Christians should be separated from the Muslims who consider it a violation of their religion to have any (Christian) political authority over them.[27] In other words, Christians should have their own house of assembly, senate and other political bodies which Muslims have—that is, a separate government.

All of the above challenges and requests have little to do with the establishment and application of Islamic law. Christians are just politically motivated to seek support for Christians, and to vent their anger against Islamic law application and Muslims. However, it should be pointed out that not all Christian denominations and organizations subscribe to the above demands, as pointed out by Ludwig, Frieder in his article.[28] Yet both Muslim and Christian politicians take the advantage of these conflicts between Christianity and Islam to manipulate their members and advance their "selfish" cause by soliciting help from abroad.

Furthermore, in Nigeria, such a rereading of "ordinary" communal conflict offers a good return to the politicians who can peddle it effectively: Christians can call on aid from the USA, whereas ambitious Muslim leaders can turn to the Middle East or sometimes North Africa for funds. Successful appeals for help only tend to confirm the original analysis as the funding reinforces Christian and Muslim groups and helps them to feel "embattled": they are then ready to diagnose any hotspot or any nascent dispute as "religious" at its root. [29]

Regarding the request to sponsor Christian pilgrims to the Holy Land in Jerusalem, the government finally funded them, while some *Shari`ah* states succumbed to the pressure from their Christian members and established the Christian Pilgrim Board, despite the fact that such visits to Rome or Jerusalem are not required religiously. The idea was politically motivated. Christians do not like the idea that Muslims are able to visit Mecca every year.[30] Thousands of Muslims perform pilgrimage annually, and the government finds it necessary to cater to their health and welfare during the Hajj. That was what initially led to the establishment of the Nigerian Pilgrim Board. At present, thousands of Muslims continue to visit Mecca annually while the number of Christians visiting Jerusalem is decreasing because it is not part of their religion. One wonders, too, what such pilgrimage has to do with the application of Islamic law. Regardless, the government has resolved the issue amicably and established two pilgrim boards: the Muslim Pilgrim Board and the Christian Pilgrim Board. However, J. H. Boer laments Christian attitudes in their demand for everything that Muslims request. He questions their demands and where they draw the line between religion and state/politics in the so-called Nigerian secular state. He says:

> On the one hand, Christians denounce government involvement in Muslim affairs such as the annual pilgrimage, in Muslim universities or university departments thinly disguised as centers for Arabic studies, in the building of mosques and in unilateral support for Muslim radio programing. These are private and spiritual matters in which the government has no business, Christians argue. But then they turn around and demand government support for their schools and hospitals ... The only disagreement Christians had with respect to the grants for the national ecumenical center is that it was not enough. They have even forced the hand of government to support Christian pilgrimages to Rome and Jerusalem so that many states have two pilgrim boards, one for Christians, the other for Muslims. Christians hover haltingly between a secular approach and pluralism or multi-religion.[31]

In this quotation, Boer criticizes Christians' double standards. On one hand they are saying that Nigeria is a secular state and thus should not sponsor any religion; on the other hand, they are demanding that the Nigerian government sponsors their own projects and institutions because they are supporting Muslims on their pilgrimage to Mecca.

With regard to the restoration of the diplomatic relationship with the State of Israel, the relationship was based purely on politics. The federal government inclined towards Egypt since the Biafran War because of the military assistance and training that the Nigerian Air Force received from Egypt during that war. Thus after the war between Israel and Egypt in 1973, the Nigerian government was encouraged by the Arab leaders, particularly the president of Egypt, to cut diplomatic ties with the State of Israel and it did. This issue provoked bitter comments and controversy in Nigeria, particularly among southerners. However, under pressure from the Christians, diplomatic relations were restored in 1996. At present, both countries maintain embassies in Lagos, Abuja and Tel-Aviv. President Goodluck, Jonathan's visit to Israel in 2013 strengthened the relationship between the countries. The CAN wanted to make a point with this issue, otherwise the restoration of diplomatic relations between Israel and Nigeria has nothing to do with the application of the *Shari`ah* in Nigeria.[32]

On the issue of paying a salary to Christian mediators who help to resolve domestic and family issues, Muslim advocates of the *Shari`ah* have responded to it adequately, as mentioned by Kenny.[33] It should be pointed out that Muslim imams are not paid by the government. Serving as an imam is an act of piety and devotion to the Muslim community. Generally, imams do not receive any official support from the government. Occasionally, those who act as imams and teachers for children or the community earn a salary or receive gifts for their teaching, which is considered to be an extra job, from parents or philanthropists. The Imams in the army who receive salaries are recruited as chaplains, just like Christian chaplains.

Regarding the acquisition of land to build churches, the government does not sell land; individuals do. Where there is a necessity to build religious buildings in any government facilities, such as airports, universities and government secretariats, the government grants all religious groups a piece of land where they can build adjacent to one another. For instance, in Lagos, Ibadan, Jos and Kaduna, the churches and mosques are built in the same area on university campuses. Thus the idea that the government does not grant land for building churches is inaccurate. As for the destruction of houses of God, both Muslims and Christians destroy the others' temples as a result of local tensions. Some Muslims in the north destroy churches; some Christians in the Middle Belt and in the east destroy Muslim mosques.[34] And at times in the same city, they destroy each others' properties, as happened in Plateau State. Religion has little to do with such actions—these are based purely on tribal racism and rooted disagreement. Muslims and Christians should learn to live together peacefully without tension.[35] Leaders of both religions should engage in fruitful dialogue to understand one another. Both religions teach peace and compassion, so both should put this into action and think of how to help one another to live side by side in harmony.

There are a few other issues which some scholars relate to the discussion of the application of Islamic law in Nigeria, such as Nigeria's membership of the Organization of Islamic Conference in Saudi-Arabia. I see these issues as irrelevant to the application of Islamic law and therefore do not address them here.

Conclusion

From the above discussion it is clear that Christians' critique of the application of the *Shari`ah* focuses on the negative side of the conflicts as if there had never been any cooperation between Muslims and Christians in Nigeria before the debate on the *Shari`ah*, or as if the *Shari`ah* appeared accidentally in Nigerian politics. Islamic law arose in the country centuries before the arrival of the British colonial invaders. Muslims and Christians have lived for decades, accommodating one another, intermarried with one another and compromising on several social issues prior to the 1960s and 1970s, when the *Shari`ah* again became the focus of public debate. To concentrate on the negative aspects of the *Shari`ah* is an unreasonable approach, as pointed out by Ludwig, Frieder in his work:

> But to focus exclusively on clashes and chaos (as does Joseph Kenny in his article on Sharia and Christianity in Nigeria) leads to a one-sided and cynical view which does not do justice to the complex relationship between Muslims and Christians in Nigeria either.[36]

Indeed, the discord between Muslim advocates of the *Shari`ah* and the CAN's opposition is not as devastating as projected by the media and by some scholars. While many Christians object to the full application of Islamic law and perceive it as an attempt to achieve Islamization, a few Christian leaders and some members of the CAN welcome the ban on acitivities involving, for example, alcohol, gambling, sex commercialization and homosexuality, which they consider to be evil. God in Islam and Christianity demands moral order and the shunning of evil.

In addition, the level of application of Islamic law in the north differs from one state to another. A great deal of concession and compromises are made steadily and gradually as needed to accommodate non-Muslims so as not to eliminate or humiliate them. As the implementation of Islamic law advances and grows, both Muslims and Christians begin to understand one another and initiate dialogue among them, which proves successful in reducing unnecessary tension. Readers should recognize that the social, political and economic problems that Nigerians face on daily basis are not the result of the application of Islamic law but are generated as a result of a lack of good leadership, together with poor management of the country's natural and human resources. Regardless of the differences and problems, Muslims and Christians in Northern Nigeria should work together to bring everlasting peace to the country; no one group can do it alone and no one group would leave the country for another group. Nigerian Muslims and Christians are unavoidably neighbors. They have to live together harmoniously. They should learn from the Yoruba people's experience of coexistence with many religious groups: Muslims, Christians and followers of traditional native religions. Among the Yorubas, families have members of all of the main religions: a father may be a Muslim and his wife a Christian, while his uncles and aunts are followers of African Traditional Religions. Children do not always embrace the religions of their parents; they choose for themselves and they intermarry with other religious groups. Conversion from one religion to another is common and converts are not subject to any penalty or castigation.[37]

Notes

1. It is interesting to learn that some Christians have converted to Islam and some Muslims who were exiled to Ethiopia became Christians. None was penalized for their conversion. This is the nature of coexistence. For more information about this, see Muhammad Husayn Haykal, *The Life of Muhammad*, translated by Ismail Ragi al Faruqi (Indiana, Plainfiel: American Trust Publication, 1976). See also Sulayman S. Nyang, *Islam in the United States of America* (Chicago: ABC International Group, Inc., 1999), p. 117.
2. Mahmoud Ayoub, "Roots of Muslim-Christian Conflicts," in *The Muslim World*, vol. 79, (Jan 1989): 25–45.
3. From the Council of Florence (1438–1445) "Decree for the Jacobites, *The Church Teaches: Documents of the Church in English* Translation, ed. And trans., John F. Clarkson, John H. Edwards, William J. Kelley and John J. Welch (St. Louis: B. Herder Book Co., 1955), p. 78 [#165].
4. Bernard Lewis, *Islam and the West* (New York: Oxford University Press, 1993, p. 17.
5. Until recently, the relationship between the Roman Catholics (the major sect of Christianity) and non-Christians has not been very cordial. However, the current pope, Francis, is making great efforts to forge good relationships with non-Christians all over the world. Muslims have welcomed his call for coexistence.
6. Akintunde Akinade, *Christian Responses to Islam in Nigeria: A Contextual Study of Ambivalent Encounters*. (N.Y.: Palgrave Macmillan, 2014), pp. 107–109; see also Murray Last's article, "Muslims and Christians in Nigeria: An Economy of Political Panic," in *The Round Table*, vol. 96, no. 392 (October 2007): 605–616. M. Last confirms the fact that Muslims and Christians have lived together in Nigeria peacefully for more than a

century. He points out that despite this harmonious engagement between these two religions, they have occasionally killed one another and destroyed the other's property in Nigeria for one reason or another.

7. Experience has shown that wherever the British occupied, Christian missionaries ran the schools for the empire. Being in charge of education, they propagated Christianity and converted the conquered people to Christianity. These missionaries believe that they are "saving" souls.
8. Of course, there were some foreign missionaries who were impressed by the Muslim attitude toward Islam and their non-aggressive efforts to preach their religions peacefully to their neighbors. See Akinade, p. 108.
9. For more information about the difference between law and morality, see Sanjib Kumar's article at http://www.publishyourarticles.net/knowledge-hub/law/what-is-the-difference-between-law-and-morality/4207 (accessed on May 11, 2016). He analyzes twelve differences between law and morality. What we find in the New Testament is moral injunctions. See also Brian Lewis' article "Morality and Law." He explains the true nature and understanding of law in Christianity: http://v2catholic.com/blewis/2012/2012-06. (Accessed on May 11, 2016).
10. Frieder Ludwig, "Christian Muslim Relations in Northern Nigeria since the Introduction of *Shari`ah* in 1999," *Journal of the American Academy of Religion,* vol. 76, no 3 (September 2008): 602–637. See p. 603.
11. Ibid., p. 603. Ludwig, Frieder references Mazrui, Ali as saying that the reintroduction of Islamic law in Nigeria should not be seen as means of Islamization but as "an element of the cultural 'self-determination' of a 'non-Western people'." Mazrui, Ali argues that Nigeria is the only African country outside Arab Africa which has seriously debated an alternative to the Western constitutional and legal option. See Ludwig, Frieder, p. 605. Mazrui, Ali asserts that the *Shari`ah* only leads to a pluralistic society and not to a society that follows one legal system. It is surprising that Christians object to the Islamization of Nigeria when from the beginning of Christianity's arrival in Nigeria, missionaries from all over the worldwent to Nigeria to Christianize the country by all means possible. Ethel Miller, who waged relentless attacks against Islam, Muhammad and Muslims, was a foreign Christian missionary in Northern Nigeria. Her aim was to Christianize the country. She was frustrated by the British colonial ban on evangelization in the north. She defied it and continued to preach Christianity to Muslims there. See Andrew Barnes' article "Religious Insult: Christian Critiques of Islam and the Government in Colonial Northern Nigeria," *Journal of Religion in Africa,* vol. 34, no 1&2 (Feb–May, 2004): 62–81. For more information about Christian missionary activities to Christianize Nigeria, see Mujahid Hamza Shitu, "A Review of the Activities of Christian Missionary, Clergy, Experts and Writers on Islam

in Nigeria," *Journal of Islamic Studies and Culture*, vol. 2, no. 3 (September 2014): 25–46.

12. Some people in Nigeria still believe that the federal government should be divided into two states: northern and southern. It was on that basis that Ojukwu attempted to separate Biafra from Nigeria in 1967. The followers of Ojukwu today are still hoping to form a separate government of their own in Eastern Nigeria.
13. Kenney Joseph, "Sharia and Christianity in Nigeria: Islam and a Secular State," *Journal of Religion in Africa*, vol. 26, no. 4, (Nov. 1996): 338–364. (See p. 347.)
14. Kenny quotes Shani in the daily paper *New Nigeria* of August 30, 1977.
15. Kenny, p. 347.
16. Some Christians in Kaduna, Gombe and Katsina states had threatened that they would establish their own Christian laws if the *Shari`ah* was applied to them. However, the government in these states was able to settle the matter amicably and thus Christians and Muslims now work together.
17. Ludwig Frieder, p. 632.
18. Kenny, p. 348.
19. Akintunde Akinade, *Christian Responses to Islam in Nigeria: A Contextual Study of Ambivalent Encounters.* UK: Palgrave, Macmillan, 2014, pp. 124–125.
20. Ludwig, p. 603.
21. Akinade, pp. 107–109. He mentions how Ajayi Crowder, a Yoruba missionary, was received by Muslims in Yorubaland and in Jebba.
22. See Ezekiel 18:20: "The son shall not suffer for the iniquity of the father nor the father suffers for the iniquity of the son."
23. The story of Adam eating from the forbidden tree is mentioned in chapter 2 and 7 in detail in the *Qur'an*. Then he repented and sought forgiveness from God, and he was forgiven.
24. The orientalists are the European scholars who study the orient—Eastern people, Asians and Arabs. Orientalism is the scholarly study and knowledge of Asian culture, languages and people. It is the study of others as opposite. See Wikipedia on orientalism. See also *Orientalism* by Edward Said.
25. There are many books on Islam. Readers who want to learn more should read John Esposito's *Islam: The Straight Path.* Oxford: Oxford Press, 2015 new edition, and Yushau Sodiq's *An Insider's Guide to Islam.* Indianapolis, Trafford Publishing, 2010. Mujahid Shitu in his article traces back the idea of labeling Islam with bad names to John of Damascus in the seventh century and how Christians tried to discredit Islam and its beliefs.
26. Kenny, pp. 348–349.
27. Kenny, p. 349.

28. Ludwig Frieder points out that not all aspects of the *Shari`ah* are repugnant to all Christians in Nigeria. He refers to the abovementioned resistance as "selective resistance" by some Christians (p. 616). Those Christians who supported the *Shari`ah* argue that the ban on alcohol, gambling and other activities are also sanctioned in the Bible but not implemented. The *Shari`ah* in this sense would keep the society free from a lot of social evils.
29. See Murray Last's article, p. 606. There are several cases to support Last's idea here. During the Biafra War, the Christian east turned to the British for support, and the northern Muslims turned to Arabs for support. This civil war was turned into religious war even though the head of the Nigerian government then was Yakubu Gowon, a Christian from the north, who is known to have inaugurated the policy of "eat and let others eat."
30. Without doubt, Muslims' visits to Mecca allow them to be exposed to other cultures, to meet other Muslims from around the world and to communicate with them. It gives them ample opportunity to engage in intellectual exchanges with other Muslims. When Muslims return from Mecca, they earn the title of "al-Hajj," which is a badge of honor for them. Pilgrimage opens doors for Muslims to trade with the Arab countries.
31. Ludwig, Frieder, pp. 616–617, quoting Jan Boar in "The Nigerian Christian – Muslim Standoff: Some Underlying Issues, Parameters for a Solution," *TCNN Research Bulletin,* 33/200 (40th Anniversary Issue):4–23.
32. Even though Israel is a secular state, the ultraorthodox members of the Knesset exercise great control over Israel's parliament.
33. Ibid, pp. 349–350.
34. See Murray Last's article.
35. For more information about why Muslims and Christians should live together, Akinade's *Christian Responses to Islam in Nigeria* is a must-read. After narrating the tension between Muslims and Christians, he suggests several ways of developing inter-religious dialogue so that both could live together peacefully as they are created to do. I would add to that by emphasizing that the decision of who goes to heaven or hell should be left to God. No one religion has a monopoly of heaven, despite the claim of many traditions to do so.
36. LudwigLudwig, Frieder, p. 606.
37. Murray Last, pp. 606–607. The author of this article is from Southern Nigeria. His parents are converts to Islam, some of his brothers are Christians and some of his sisters are followers of African Traditional Religions, yet they all live under one roof. Some attend missionary schools and others attend Arabic schools, but all are sponsored by the same parents. They all live together peacefully and love one another.

CHAPTER 6

Is the Application of Islamic Law in Zamfara State a Success or a Failure?

Introduction

I shall begin this chapter with a quote from Aliyu Musa Yawuri, who has done extensive research on the implementation of Islamic law in Nigeria. He says:

> Nigerian Muslims are deeply committed to their religion; that explains the massive support the Muslims gave to the recent implementation of the Sharia criminal justice system in the North. Multiplicity of culture, ethnicity and religion created a divide, which in turn created mutual suspicion largely between the Muslims and Christians. I think it is this suspicion that moved a section of the Christians in the North to view the introduction of Sharia as a holy jihad designed to culminate in the eventual dethronement of the secular nature of Nigeria. The Muslim on the other hand nurses a certain fear of concerted designs by some persons within and outside the country to truncate the implementation of Sharia. The result being, when the Christian opines that the implementation of Sharia is unconstitutional, the Muslims view this opinion as a move to destroy Sharia.[1]

In this quotation he elucidates the nature of religion among Nigerians, and how each group cherishes its religion and is ready to adhere to and practice such beliefs in their daily lives. He expresses the feelings of the Muslims regarding the application of Islamic law and the fear of the Christians about it. These emotions generate suspicion and breed tension between these two, the largest religious groups in Nigeria.

Y. Sodiq, *A History of the Application of Islamic Law in Nigeria*,
DOI 10.1007/978-3-319-50600-5_6

In this chapter I shall analyze the application of Islamic law in Zamfara State, evaluating whether its application is successful or unsuccessful and the effect of its application on the people of Zamfara State.[2] Hence this chapter is a case study.

As pointed out at the beginning of this book, Nigeria is a country of diverse cultures. Wherever one goes in the world, one finds Nigerians. However, the Nigerian government is fraught with corruption, social ills, moral decadence and an unstable environment, particularly the tension in Delta region and the Boko Haram in the north. The hopes of the people were high when President Muhammad Buhari took over as an elected civilian leader in May 29, 2015. Fortunately or unfortunately, it was during the reign of the former presider, Olusegun Obasanjo that twelve states from Northern Nigeria opted for the application of Islamic law in their states. It was a shock to many Nigerians. President Obasanjo insisted then that Nigeria is a democratic government and therefore each state has the right to choose the laws it wants among existing legal systems in Nigeria: common law, native law and Islamic law.

In this chapter I address how the application of Islamic law was reintroduced in Zamfara State, what areas Islamic law covered and why, how it has been implemented, and the effects of its implementation on the people of Zamfara. Even though many people hear about Northern Nigeria, they know little about its legal systems. Hence, when the governor of Zamfara State, Ahmad Thani Yerima, declared that he would apply Islamic law there, many Nigerians objected to it, thinking that it was unconstitutional to do so. Nevertheless, both parties presented their arguments rationally and emotionally. Finally these northern states went ahead and applied Islamic law because it was what the majority of their citizens wanted and, since democratic government is a system which respects individual decisions, the *Shari`ah* is allowed to stay. To what extent does the law affect the northerners who apply Islamic law upon their citizens? Are the people in the north who practice Islamic law more secure than others? Are they better off economically and politically? Is justice being achieved in these states? Are the majority of the citizens happy with the application of the *Shari`ah*? Are non-Muslims oppressed by Islamic law? Are their rights as citizens being respected and protected? These are a few questions that come to mind whenever the issue of the application of Islamic law is raised and discussed. Not all them will be answered here. This chapter only addresses the question of the effect of the application of Islamic law on the people of Zamfara State.[3]

When the British conquered the Sokoto Caliphate in 1903, to its surprise it found an established legal system of governance. It was a shock to the British to find that the Fulani and Hausa were civilized, literate and organized. They all had systems of governance, the judiciary, the police, a tax system, and effective administration and documentation of their proceedings. Hence the British had no choice but to rule them through their own leaders. They established an indirect rule policy whereby the local leaders remained in charge of their own people and the British oversaw their activities, offering advice where necessary. As a result, the northerners were left alone to apply Islamic law on their people. At that particular time in Nigeria, the southerners (the Yorubas and the Ibos) had no written law and no systematic judicial procedures. Native leaders and kings (the Obas) assumed the role of executing justice among their people. They had no documentation. In fact, most Yorubas and Ibos then were illiterate. The only literate people among them were the Muslim scholars who could read Arabic and Ajami script. After a short period the British government began to interfere and make changes to the application of Islamic law. It recognized some laws and abrogated others on the pretext that they were harsh and repugnant to natural justice. It abolished some of the *hudud* laws (Islamic criminal codes), such as stoning to death for adultery, cutting off a thief's hand, and persecution of murderers and armed robbers. The abolition of these laws led to the erosion of security and social values in the north. Later, a new penal code was established for Northern Nigeria. It was endorsed and applied until after independence. Yet many people were not satisfied with the changes by the British. They hoped that one day they would be able to re-establish and reapply Islamic law in its entirety. Thus, after independence in 1960, the northerners kept pressing for the application of Islamic law in their states, and gradually and steadily they continued to win support for it until finally, in 2000, many opted for the wholesale application of the *Shari`ah*. They went to their state house of assembly, which wholeheartedly voted for Islamic law. The northern states set in motion the procedures to apply the *Shari`ah*. They hired qualified lawyers, judges and administrators to help them implement Islamic law and expand it to all areas of life. A new Islamic penal code was enacted in each state.

The establishment or adoption of the *Shari`ah* in twelve northern states caused uproar and intense criticism of Islamic law in Nigeria and abroad. The opponents alleged that the application of Islamic law is unconstitutional because it amounts to recognition of and giving preference to a religious law over the Constitution of the Federal Republic of Nigeria, and by implication it amounts to the rejection of the Constitution as the supreme law of the country. Opponents believed that the states that opted for Islamic law were politically motivated and that they would soon abandon the quest for implementing Islamic law. Both proponents and exponents of Islamic law argued back and forth, but finally the Islamic law was endorsed in twelve states as the supreme law of those states. However, the level of application of the law differs from one state to another, and the procedure is also different.

A Short History of Zamfara State

Zamfara is one of the old Hausa states of Northern Nigeria. It was part of Sokoto State until it was partitioned as a new state in 1996 under the military regime of Sanni Abasha. It has a population of about 3 million people and its capital is Gusau. Its inhabitants are mostly Hausa and Fulani, with minority Ibos, Yoruba, Nupe and Tivs. English is the official language but people speak Hausa, Fulfude and Arabic in their daily lives. Islam is the main religion of the people, with minority Christians and a few traditional religions. When the military regime fell and a civil government came to power in 1999, the then newly democratically elected president, Olusegun Obasanjo, enacted a new constitution. Under this, each state was allowed to choose the legal system it preferred to apply. This gave the governor of Zamfara State, Ahmad Sanni Yerima, the chance to opt for the full application of Islamic law in all aspects of life, including criminal law. On October 27, 1999, Zamfara State's governor announced publicly that his state would apply the *Shari`ah*, that the Zamfara house of assembly had approved the motion and that the application would take effect on January 27, 2000. It did. The announcement caused an uproar in the media and government within Nigeria and abroad.

Before the federal government could take action for or against it, a few states in the north announced their readiness to follow suit. In 2000–2001, the following states had declared their commitment to applying Islamic law: Bauchi State in June 2001, Bornu State in June 2001, Gombe State in November 2001, Jigawa State in August 2000, Kaduna State in November 2001, Kano State in November 2000, Katsina State in August 2000, Kebbi State in December 2000, Niger State in early 2000, Sokoto State in January 2001 and Yobe State in October 2001.[4] However, not all of them endorsed the application of Islamic law in its entirety. For instance, Kaduna and

Bauchi states did not approve the wholesale application of Islamic law in all aspects of life; they allowed the Christians in their states the right to be adjudicated by Christian customary laws in area courts. Any case which involved Muslims and Christians were heard by the magistrates' courts, except when both parties agreed to be adjudicated by *Shari`ah* courts, which sometimes happened. Even Zamfara State, which spearheaded the application of Islamic law, did not officially endorse the application of the law of apostasy because of its sensitivity and the damage its application might cause to Islam and Muslims' image in a country which prides itself on being democratic. Nigeria guarantees freedom of religion to all of its citizens. Any endorsement of the law of apostasy would go against that great foundation.

From 2000, twelve states began to apply Islamic law. One may ask, are these states more secured today due to the application of Islamic penal codes? Are the people of these states and Zamfara in particular better off economically as a result of this application? Are the citizens of Zamfara happy with the result of this application? What are the major achievements of the government after it had applied this law for ten years and more? How were non-Muslims being treated in Zamfara State? What did non-Muslims feel about this application? Were they discriminated against? Were they being relegated to second-class citizens? Did they receive fair treatment from state government and apparatus? Did the government actually assess its performance from the beginning of the application of the *Shari`ah*? What is the future of Islamic law in Zamfara State? Few data are available to help answer these important questions.

Starting from the last question, it appears that Zamfara State will continue to apply the *Shari`ah* regardless of what negative responses it receives from the people. The advocates of this application believe very strongly that Nigerians will embrace and admire the achievements of Islamic law as time goes on. For any law to be embraced and successful, they believe, it will take time, sacrifices, adjustments and modifications. As they apply it, they will learn from their mistakes and so they are adamant about its application. There is no thought whatsoever that the application of Islamic law will disappear in the north; rather, there is great potential that other states in Nigeria will opt for the application of Islamic law to please their constituencies. It seems to me that the northerners care little about the reality of the complexity of the law; they are guided by the perception of living under its rule. Politically and economically, they are bankrupt with this application, but they are emotionally satisfied with it and that is all they are interested in, in my opinion.

Accusation Against the Application of Islamic Law in Zamfara State

While the advocates of Islamic law make big claims of significant achievements in terms of security and economy as a result of its application, critics have pointed out many areas where the law has failed. They argue that the application has not achieved any substantial positive goals but rather caused havoc for the people of Zamfara State.

The first accusation was the idea that because of the need to apply Islamic law, Zamfara State became a police state where the government established the *Hisbah* group to monitor and enforce *Shari`ah*. The group is perceived as a moral religious police force, which *can* accuse and hold people responsible for their actions. Though *Hisbah* does not have any authority like the federal police to detain offenders, it has been charged with the power to suspect and charge people for moral violations of the Islamic code. Since it has more interaction with locals and it does not have a uniform, its members are able to mingle with the public and charge suspected people, probably arbitrarily. As a result, citizens of Zamfara feel that they have been robbed of their constitutional freedom to do what they want without being policed. People occasionally accuse *Hisbah* of abuses of its power. At times it has conflicts with the federal police. Of course, several attempts by the state and federal police have been made to unify their efforts. The police perceives *Hisbah* as a rival for its authority.

Another strong accusation was the challenge of discrimination against non-Muslims in many areas, especially in the economy. While the advocates of Islamic law insist on banning the selling of alcohol publicly, Christians, whose religion does not condemn its selling and drinking, were banned from operating publicly, so they lost many customers. Many beer parlors were closed because of the government's ban on alcohol. What Muslims consider a gain amounts to a great loss for Christian traders. The advocates of Islamic law have pledged that it will not be applied to Christians and other non-Muslims, but the ban on alcohol has serious negative effects on these groups. Those few Christians who insist on opening their beer parlors in their homes and selling beer and other alcoholic beverages are perceived as immoral people by *Hisbah.* They are labeled as enemies of progress. Zamfara State also bans gambling, prostitution and whatever it terms immoral activities. The majority of the people who operate these businesses are Christians from the southern and eastern parts of Nigeria. They suffer economic loss as a result of this ban.

Through the application of Islamic law, the state also bans the use of the same bus by males and females, hence the birth of segregation of the sexes in transportation. As a result, there was a drastic drop in the numbers of people using public transport, which resulted in a decline in businesses in the state. Again, the majority of taxi drivers and *okada* drivers in Zamfara and many northern states are non-Muslims. They expressed their frustration with the ban. Later, the government bought buses for women's transportation,[5] but these do not carry women who aren't wearing the *Hijab*, which is another frustrating issue.

Further, the advocates of Islamic law are accused of immoral discrimination against the poor. If a poor person violates the *Shari`ah*, the law is applied to them. However, if a rich person breaks the law, the *Shari`ah* is not adequately applied, the punishment is reduced or the law is reinterpreted. Hence the hands of those who stole cows and donkeys worth 20,000 naira or less were cut off, while those who stole millions of naira from the state's treasury escaped the punishment on a legal technicality in court. Nonetheless, no victim has been stoned to death in Zamfara State despite the fact that the law prescribes stoning to death for adultery.

Lastly, women are directly or indirectly kept at home by insisting that their legitimate roles as mothers lie there and not in the public arena. Therefore only a few participate in public work or hold government positions in the state. Women are perceived as being discriminated against in public. They are excluded from holding ministerial, political and leadership positions. Zamfara State is accused of denying business permission to non-Muslims there. This is done under different pretexts, such as a lack of adequate information.

It is alleged, too, that Zamfara remains less prosperous economically because of the application of Islamic law. Most of the trades that brought money to the state have been stopped. Alcohol and gambling have been banned and stage entertainment discouraged. Women (more than half of the population) are relegated to home duties, such as cooking and nursing, so they are not able to contribute to the development of the state economically. They remain consumers and recipients rather than producers. If such a trend of the degradation of women continues, the state will not develop technically and economically because half of the population merely consumes and does not produce. However, Zamfara State officials deny these accusations, arguing that they are misconceptions and prejudice against Islamic law. Everything leveled against Zamfara State can equally be leveled against any state in the eastern and southern regions of Nigeria, which do not practice Islamic law.

The Claim of the Achievements of Applying Islamic Law

Every year since 2001, each northern state which applies Islamic law has claimed victory and celebrated its achievements and prosperity. But what exactly do these states realistically achieve? Indeed, it is hard to pinpoint any specific achievement except for the general claims which each state makes. Attempts to obtain statistics on the achievements of these states have not been successful.[6] There are a few papers that have been presented at conferences in Nigeria on the *Shari`ah* in which the authors assert the achievements of the application of Islamic law but without providing data to support their claims. In addition, much of what is claimed to be offered to the citizens of Zamfara State are basic things that citizens are entitled to receive anyway. For instance, Shehu U. D. Keffi mentions in "Improving the Quality of Life Through the Implementation of Social-Economic Aspects of *Shari`ah* in Nigeria"[7] that Zamfara State offered loans to many groups in Zamfara to alleviate poverty among citizens. This, in my view, falls within the responsibility of the state to assist the needy and implementation of the *Shari`ah* has little to do with it. The federal government establishes different agencies to eradicate poverty in Nigeria, among both Muslims and non-Muslims. The federal and state governments often provide "soft loans" to various groups with the aim of helping them to tackle poverty. This has never been an exclusive duty of the *Shari`ah* states.

However, it should be pointed out here that Zamfara State established the institution of *Zakat*,[8] which is charged with collection of *Zakat*, gift and endowment and their distribution to the needy members of society. This institution of *Zakat* differs from taxes which the federal and state agencies collect from citizens. Not so apparent is whether or not the *Zakat* money has ever been utilized to support all citizens in the state. Also, we do not know whether non-Muslims ever received support from the *Zakat* money. Zamfara State also claims that in an effort to implement the *Shari`ah*, it established *Hisbah*, which, according to the state, has assisted tremendously in enforcing *Shari`ah* injunctions and encouraging Zamfara citizens to abide by the *Shari`ah*. Consequently the state has become safe (in terms of crime) through the supervision of *Hisbah*. This claim could be true, but there is no data to substantiate it. However, on the other hand, using religious police creates fear among the people. Instead of using education to keep citizens informed about the financial support they can and cannot receive from the government, and the viability of Islamic law for the people, the state uses *Hisbah* to monitor people which produces negative result. By using *Hisbah* to enforce religious laws, some people become hypocritical in that they abide by the law publicly but violate it privately. This occasionally happens with regard to the consumption of alcohol in public. However, the government, which recruits *Hisbah* members, believes that it helps to check public bribery and other corrupt financial activities, such as hoarding goods to promote unnecessary inflation. *Hisbah* assists traders in improving their attitude and in using scales for trade. It also helps to find lost property at the market, according to the government.

Another achievement which the advocates of the *Shari`ah* claim is the quick dispensation of justice. Cases are taken to the courts immediately and adjudicated as quickly as possible, except for criminal cases, which often take a long time owing to the need for thorough investigation and cross-examination of evidence before making any judgment to avoid mistakes. In many of the cases that go to Islamic courts, lawyers aren't involved, so they can be resolved quickly. Many people, including some non-Muslims, prefer to take their cases to the *Shari`ah* courts because they believe that they will receive a fair judgment while having to spend less on lawyers. Adjudication in the *Shari`ah* courts also saves time for all people involved because the cases are less likely to be postponed. While many are happy with this quick dispensation, a few are skeptical about unfair rulings owing to the lack of thorough deliberation before pronouncing the final judgment/verdict.

In addition, the state legal agencies have recorded fewer court cases since the implementation of the *Shari`ah* because people resort to solving their family disputes and domestic problems through arbitration. The government encourages this. It is claimed that *Hisbah* are instrumental in carrying out arbitration among members of the community who are in dispute. Of course, if the parties involved cannot reach an amicable solution, they can still take their case to court. It should be pointed out that any party that does not agree with the judgment of the Islamic court in the state can appeal to the state high court, which is not an Islamic court. And even if they disagree with the decision of the state high court, they can still appeal to the federal court of appeal in Kaduna, which is the final resort for any disputed case, be it civil or criminal. The judges at the federal court of appeal are well versed in both common and Islamic law.

The advocates of the *Shari`ah* also claim that assistance is given to orphans across the state. While such efforts certainly help the poor, they may turn the government into a welfare state in which some citizens dishonestly claim to be orphans purely to receive government financial aid.

That would place a big financial burden on the government. Again, supporting needy members of the state is a responsibility of the government regardless of whether it applies Islamic law or not. If the government fails to help orphans or any people in need, they will resort to violence or crime and become irresponsible citizens. What the government then spends to put them in prison will be more than what it would have spent to keep them as responsible members of the society.

Further, the *Shari`ah* advocates argue that the judges are receiving intensive training to implement Islamic law. In my view, this is a great achievement because if the judges receive adequate training, they will be able to discharge their duties fairly and deliver equitable justice; the community will thus trust the judiciary. The *Shari`ah* courts prior to the partition of Zamfara State from Sokoto State were at times suspected of discrimination against non-Muslims. What should be understood from these claims is that the application of the *Shari`ah* is not limited to legal issues but spreads to all aspects of Muslims' daily lives, both private and public. Therefore, the advocates of the *Shari`ah* perceive any function that the state performs or any project it implements as part and parcel of the promotion of Islamic law and Islamic values. The main objective of the advocates of the *Shari`ah* is to Islamize the state because that is what the majority of Zamfara citizens want. Non-Muslims object to this religious motive and agenda of proselytization.

Zamfara State also claims that all of its citizens are treated equally without discrimination. However, such a claim has no substance because both Yorubas and Ibos, who reside in the state, are labeled foreigners and treated as others. Hence the state offers them special financial assistance as soft loans to improve their situation. This is pointed out by Sheikh Keffi in his article.[9] The very fact that Yorubas and Ibos are singled out for assistance amounts to discrimination. They are assisted because they are not entitled to what Zamfara citizens are entitled to. There are many Yorubas and Ibos who were born and raised in Zamfara, yet they could not stand for any government or ministerial positions because the leaders of Zamfara's government perceive them as aliens despite the fact that they and their parents were born in Zamfara and they are Nigerians. Even though such discrimination against non-indigenous people is common in Nigeria, it is an unIslamic practice. Zamfara State should not allow this because it claims to be following Islamic law, which recognizes all believers as equal (*Qur'an* ch 49:13) who must therefore be treated with dignity, fairness and respect. One wonders when a Yoruba Muslim, who was born and raised in Zamfara, would be seen as an indigenous person who could legitimately hold a high governmental position and be elected as a senator, governor or member of the house of assembly.

Some Observations

It appears from the above analysis that many claims of achievement by Zamfara State are questionable to say the least. The claim of better public safety lacks concrete data and convincing evidence. The claim of better and equal treatment of all citizens is contested by non-Muslims and Yoruba Muslims, who allege social, economic and political discrimination against them. The claim of economic advancement has not been proved, even though the government has spent billions of naira on various developmental projects whose results have yet to be seen.

However, one area in which Zamfara State should be given credit is in the ban on alcohol consumption and drug abuse. If the citizens abided by it, there would be a great reduction in domestic violence and traffic accidents regardless of whether they are Muslims or not. Again, there is no statistical data available to substantiate this claim. Documented data from other countries, such as the USA and Canada, have shown that a reduction in alcohol consumption and drug use often leads to a great reduction in accidents and domestic violence. Nonetheless, non-Muslims and traders who engage in alcohol-related and other banned businesses perceive the ban as a blow to their businesses, and some of them have actually moved out of Zamfara State while others have changed to other businesses.

On the other hand, the establishment of the *Hisbah* group, which the state believes to be instrumental in helping Muslims adhere to Islamic law, is considered to be an intrusion into the freedom of the citizens. Many people perceive *Hisbah*'s function to be that of a moral police force, so this initiative yields negative results. In addition, the support and help that the government offers its citizens are duties and responsibilities of the state and as such they have nothing to do with the application of the *Shari`ah*. That is, even if the state does not apply the *Shari`ah,* it has a duty to help the poor, the orphans, *almanjari* (professional beggars) and members of the community who are in dire need of assistance.

While the proponents of the *Shari`ah* should be given credit for their fervent attempt to root out corruption and moral vices in Zamfara State, it should be recognized that the progressive building of the state infrastructure in terms of providing resources for constructing schools and vocational institutions and offering loans to the needy are not the result of the implementation of the *Shari`ah*. These are duties which the state has a responsibility to discharge regardless of whether it applies Islamic law or common law. In fact, people elected the governor and his executive members to improve the lives and lot of the citizens. When the state constructs roads, builds hospitals or fights crime, it does so because that is its duty and responsibility: to modernize the state, educate the people and defend the citizens against any threat internally and externally. Of course, the application of the *Shari`ah* might be a deterrent to people committing more crimes. If this can be proved with empirical data then the *Shari`ah* would be given due credit.

On the other hand, the proponents of the *Shari`ah* count among their successes the assistance offered to Muslims to build mosques, and payment of a salary to the imams and muazzins (those who call believers to prayer). This can only be considered a success if other religious groups, such as Christians, receive similar support from the state. Otherwise, such exclusive support for Muslims would amount to discrimination, which breeds ill feeling among different religious groups in the state. I also believe that by paying a salary to imams the government can control the religious leaders in the society, as experience has shown in other countries, such as Saudi Arabia, Egypt and Libya. In the near future, those Imams would dance to the tune of the government and would never attempt to criticize it through fear of losing their pay checks. Such a practice is unhealthy and occasionally creates a welfare state where the majority of people depend financially on the government to survive.

Also among the successes which the proponents of the *Shari`ah* cite is the level of awareness and commitment from the civil servants in the state to the service and advancement of the state, as well as holding each one responsible and accountable in their position. As a result, the performance of an elected member is gauged according to the standard of Islam. While this may be true, we do not have any empirical evidence to support this claim. Are the members and employees in the civil service sector actually living up to this standard and thus delivering their duties in the best manner expected of them? We do not know or have any mechanism to assess this.

Further, the critics of the application of Islamic law have pointed out that it has led to many failures and shortcomings. For example:

1. There is discrimination against non-Muslims, who are not allowed to sell alcohol or engage in gambling publicly. Thus many have lost their customers and their jobs, and some have left the state.
2. Non-Muslims, in particular Christians, are not allowed to build more churches, whereas the state encourages the building of more mosques, and the imams are paid from a government fund. This fund belongs to all citizens, not to a specific group of people.
3. There is discrimination against women. No single woman has been elected or appointed to any important ministerial or senatorial positions at the time of conducting this research. Either they are assumed to be unqualified or they are not elected because they are women. In either case the government should encourage their election and educate them to become the leaders of tomorrow. Their relegation to domestic work or bearing children and taking care of the young deprives them of their due positions and rights in the society. Women should be equal citizens of the state rather than second-class citizens.
4. There is a lack of equal treatment of citizens, especially the Ibos and Yorubas. Despite the fact that many Yorubas and Ibos were born and raised in Zamfara State and some are Muslims, they are treated as foreigners and they have little say in how they are governed. They are not allowed to serve as members of the house of assembly or as senators. They do not hold any high-level government positions under the pretext that they are not indigenous to Zamfara, even though they are Nigerian, they may have been born and raised in Zamfara and some of them know no nowhere else. When Zamfara State gave them soft loans, they were perceived as others. Such discrimination is against Islam because there are many Yorubas in Zamfara who are Muslims by birth.
5. There is no female Christian minister or senator, even though they have them in Bauchi and other states in Nigeria.

Many complaints have been made by non-Muslims, who have raised their voices and feel that they have been discriminated against. Not all Muslims of Zamfara are happy with the application of Islamic law either. They may have kept silent so as not to be labeled anti-Islam or anti-progress.

Conclusion

I shall conclude this chapter with a quotation from Yadudu's article, in which he insisted on the need for serious evaluation of the achievements and of the failures of the implementation of Islamic law in all northern states in Nigeria:

> With all its attendant imperfections and difficulties, I am satisfied that it is about time we carried out wide ranging and far reaching series of empirical studies to evaluate what impact the implementation of *Shari`ah* has had in the last seven years on the societies that had embarked upon it. The results can only help us to see what sort of things we have been doing right, which ones not so well and, hopefully, lead to improvements in the delivery of its dividends particularly in socio-economic spheres and to avoid any miscarriages of justice and minimize or eliminate implicating avoidable hardship on the believers who have voluntarily submitted to the dictates of the *Shari`ah*.[10]

Yadudu wants the political leaders, public servants and other officials who are in charge of the application of the *Shari`ah* to critically evaluate their performance rather than just concentrate on detailing their material achievements, which lack empirical data.

Indeed, Zamfara State has accomplished some achievements but not as many as the advocates of the *Shari`ah* claim. There is a need for more research to be done to determine to what extent Islamic law is perceived as beneficial to the citizens of Nigeria and of Zamfara State in particular. Any question of whether the citizens are better off as a result of the application of the *Shari`ah* cannot be easily answered because of the lack of empirical evidence. Thus it would be mere conjecture at present to conclude that the application of Islamic law is a success story or a failure. If the citizens of the state feel that they like how their government applies the law to them, let them support it. After all, they know what is good for them more than anyone else. The paternalistic attitude that some outside observers have must be suspended by giving a chance to the local people to choose their legal system, be it Islamic or not. It should be added that fifteen years seems too short a time to assess the success or failure of any newly applied legal system.

From the above analysis we can conclude that Islamic law is currently going through many phases in Northern Nigeria. While some states apply it to all spheres of life, including criminal cases, there are other states which limit its application and insist on not applying it to non-Muslims. Such flexibility has reduced the tension which many Nigerians, especially southerners, have expected to cause uproar in and disintegration of the country. Above all, both Muslims and Christians should be able to live peacefully in any state in Nigeria without being discriminated against at any level. Nigeria is a country for all Nigerians, and its citizens should develop a mutual understanding of one another.

Notes

1. Aliyu Musa Yawuri "On Defending Safiyatu Husaini and Amina Lawal," in Philip Ostein and Sati Fwatshak, *Shari`ah Implementation in Northern Nigeria 1999–2006: A Sourcebook Vol. 1–V* (Ibadan, Nigeria; Spectrum Books Limited, 2007), vol. V, p. 139.
2. In 1999, Zamfara State was the first state in Northern Nigeria to announce its intention to apply Islamic law fully. Within a year, eleven other states in Northern Nigeria declared their readiness to apply Islamic law.
3. Even though I raised many questions in the introduction to this chapter, I answered only one question because many people seriously want to know the effect of the application of Islamic law on the citizens of Zamfara State because the governor of Zamfara State, Ahmad Sanni, has claimed that his state could be a role model of justice and advancement for other states if he was allowed to implement Islamic law.
4. West Africa magazine, 8-14-2002, p. 14.
5. Some Christian organizations organized car pools for female Christians and at times arranged cars and buses exclusively for them.
6. When I was conducting this research, I tried to contact members of the house of assembly in Zamfara State, but without success. I e-mailed the state's public relation officer but there was no response. All of the statistics that I gathered are from research papers presented at some conferences in Nigeria about Islamic law.
7. Sheikh U. D. Keffi, "Improving the Quality of Life of Muslims through the Implementation of Socio-Economic Aspects of Sharia in Nigeria," a paper presented at the Conference on Women's Rights and Access to Justice Under the *Sharia* in Northern Nigeria, held at Abuja on February 26–27, 2003.
8. *Zakat* is an annual duty of 2.5% which the rich people have to take out of their wealth and give to the poor. It is part and parcel of the five pillars of Islam. It is only due once a year and it is not *sadaqah* (charity), which everyone gives. *Zakat* money can be given to non-Muslim who is in need.
9. Ibid.
10. Auwalu H. Yadudu, "Evaluating the Implementation of Shariah in Nigeria: Challenges and Limiting Factors Revisited," a paper presented at the National Conference on Leadership, State & Society Under the Shari`ah in Nigeria: The Dividends. Held in Abuja, Nigeria on July 10–12, 2006.

Appendix

Sections of the Nigerian Constitution Which Relate to the Issue of Shari`ah Law

Sec. 1. (1) This Constitution is supreme and its provisions shall have binding force on the authorities and persons throughout the Federal Republic of Nigeria.

Sec. 4. (4) In addition and without prejudice to the powers conferred by subsection (2) of this section, the National Assembly shall have power to make laws with respect to the following matters, that is to say:-

(a) any matter in the Concurrent Legislative List set out in the first column of Part II of the Second Schedule to this Constitution to the extent prescribed in the second column opposite thereto; and
(b) any other matter with respect to which it is empowered to make laws in accordance with the provisions of this Constitution.

Sec. 4. (5) If any Law enacted by the House of Assembly of a State is inconsistent with any law validly made by the National Assembly, the law made by the National Assembly shall prevail, and that other Law shall, to the extent of the inconsistency, be void.

Sec. 4. (6) The legislative powers of a State of the Federation shall be vested in the House of Assembly of the State.

Y. Sodiq, *A History of the Application of Islamic Law in Nigeria*,
DOI 10.1007/978-3-319-50600-5

Sec. 4. (7) The House of Assembly of a State shall have power to make laws for the peace, order and good government of the State or any part thereof with respect to the following matters, that is to say:-

(a) any matter not included in the Exclusive Legislative List set out in Part I of the Second Schedule to this Constitution.
(b) any matter included in the Concurrent Legislative List set out in the first column of Part II of the Second Schedule to this Constitution to the extent prescribed in the second column opposite thereto; and
(c) any other matter with respect to which it is empowered to make laws in accordance with the provisions of this Constitution.

Sec. 10. The Government of the Federation or of a State shall not adopt any religion as State religion.

Sec. 36. (12) Subject as otherwise provided by this Constitution, a person shall not be convicted of a criminal offence unless that offence is defined and the penalty therefore is prescribed in a written law, and in this subsection, a written law refer to an Act of the National Assembly or a Law of a State, any subsidiary legislation or instrument under the provision of a law.

Sec. 38. (1) Every person shall be entitled to freedom of thought, conscience and religion, including freedom to change his religion or belief, and freedom (either alone or in community with others, and in public or in private) to manifest and propagate his religion or belief in worship, teaching, practice and observance.

Sec. 42. (1) A citizen of Nigeria of a particular community, ethnic group, place of origin, sex, religion or political opinion shall not, by reason only that he is such a person:-

(a) be subjected either expressly by, or in the practical application of, any law in force in Nigeria or any executive or administrative action of the government, to disabilities or restrictions to which citizens of Nigeria of other communities, ethnic groups, places of origin, sex, religions or political opinions are not made subject.

Sec. 68. (2) The President of the Senate or the Speaker of the House of Representatives, as the case may be, shall give effect to the provisions of subsection (1) of this section, so however that the President of the Senate or the Speaker of the House of Representatives or a member shall first present evidence satisfactory to the House concerned that any of the provisions of that subsection has become applicable in respect of that member.

Sec. 233. (1) The Supreme Court shall have jurisdiction, to the exclusion of any other court of law in Nigeria, to hear and determine appeals from the Court of Appeal.

Sec. 235. Without prejudice to the powers of the President or of the Governor of a state with respect to prerogative of mercy, no appeal shall lie to any other body or person from any determination of the Supreme Court.

Sec. 260. (1) There shall be a Sharia Court of Appeal of the Federal Capital Territory, Abuja.

Sec. 261. (1) The appointment of a person to the office of the Grand Kadi of the Sharia Court of Appeal of the Federal Capital Territory, Abuja shall be made by the President on the recommendation of the National.

261 (2) The appointment of a person to the office of a Kadi of the Sharia Court of Appeal shall be made by the President on the recommendation of the National Judicial Council.

261 (3) A person shall not be qualified to hold office as Grand Kadi or Kadi of the Sharia Court of Appeal of the Federal Capital Territory, Abuja unless-

(a) he is a legal practitioner in Nigeria and has so qualified for a period of not less than ten years and has obtained a recognised qualification in Islamic law from an institution acceptable to the National Judicial Council; or
(b) he has attended and has obtained a recognized qualification in Islamic law from an institution approved by the National Judicial Council and has held the qualification for a period of not less than twelve years; and

  (i) he either has considerable experience in the Practice of Islamic law, or
  (ii) he is a distinguished scholar of Islamic law.

Sec. 262. (1) The Sharia Court of Appeal shall, in addition to such other jurisdiction as may be conferred upon it by an Act of the National Assembly, exercise such appellate and supervisory jurisdiction in civil proceedings involving questions of Islamic personal law.

Sec. 275. "There shall be for any State that requires it a Sharia Court of Appeal for that State." 277. (1) The Sharia Court of Appeal of a State shall, in addition to such other jurisdiction as may be conferred upon it by the law of the State, exercise such appellate and supervisory jurisdiction in civil proceedings involving questions of Islamic personal Law which the court is competent to decide in accordance with the provisions of subsection (2) of this section.

Sec. 262. (2) For the purposes of subsection (1) of this section, the Sharia Court of Appeal shall be competent to decide:

(a) any question of Islamic personal Law regarding a marriage concluded in accordance with that Law, including a question relating to the validity or dissolution of such a marriage or a question that depends on such a marriage and relating to family relationship or the guardianship of an infant;
(b) where all the parties to the proceedings are Muslims, any question of Islamic personal Law regarding a marriage, including the validity or dissolution of that marriage, or regarding family relationship, a founding or the guarding of an infant;
(c) any question of Islamic personal Law regarding a wakf, gift, will or succession where the endower, donor, testator or deceased person is a Muslim;
(d) any question of Islamic personal Law regarding an infant, prodigal or person of unsound mind who is a Muslim or the maintenance or the guardianship of a Muslim who is physically or mentally infirm; or
(e) where all the parties to the proceedings, being Muslims, have requested the court that hears the case in the first instance to determine that case in accordance with Islamic personal law, any other question.

Sec. 287. (1) The decisions of the supreme Court shall be enforced in any part of the Federation by all authorities and persons, and by courts with subordinate jurisdiction to that of the Supreme Court.

(2) The decisions of the Court of Appeal shall be enforced in any part of the Federation by all authorities and persons, and by courts with subordinate jurisdiction to that of the Court of Appeal.

(3) The decisions of the Federal High Court, a High Court and of all other courts established by this Constitution shall be enforced in any part

of the Federation by all authorities and persons, and by other courts of law with subordinate jurisdiction to that of the Federal High Court, a High Court and those other courts, respectively.

Sec. 288. (1) In exercising his powers under the foregoing provisions of this Chapter in respect of appointments to the offices of Justice of the Supreme Court and Justices of the Courts of Appeal, the president shall have regard to the need to ensure that there are among the holders of such offices persons learned in Islamic personal law and persons learned in Customary law.

Sec. 315. (1) Subject to the provisions of this Constitution, an existing law shall have effect with such modifications as may be necessary to bring it into conformity with the provisions of this Constitution and shall be deemed to be:

(a) an Act of the National Assembly to the extent that it is a law with respect to any matter on which the National Assembly is empowered by this Constitution to make laws; and
(b) a Law made by a House of Assembly to the extent that it is a law with respect to any matter on which a House of Assembly is empowered by this Constitution to make laws.

2 (a) a person shall be deemed to be learned in Islamic personal law if he is a legal practitioner in Nigeria and has been so qualified for a period of not less than fifteen years in the case of a Justice of the Supreme Court or not less than twelve years in the case of a Justice of the Court of Appeal and has in either case obtained a recognized qualification in Islamic law from an institution acceptable to the national Judicial Council; and

(b) a person shall be deemed to be learned in Customary law if he is a legal practitioner in Nigeria and has been so qualified for a period of not less than fifteen years in the case of a Justice of the Supreme Court or not less than twelve years in the case of a Justice of the Court of Appeal and has in either case and in the opinion of the National Judicial Council considerable knowledge of and experience in the practice of Customary law.

Bibliography

Abdalati, Hammudah. 1977. *The Family Structure in Islam*. Indianapolis: American Trust Publications.

Abdullah, Umar. 1978. Malik's Concept of "*Amal*" in the Light of Maliki Legal Theory. Ph.D dissertation, University of Chicago.

Adamu, Aminu. 2008. *Zina* (Adultery) Under Islamic Law in Nigeria. In SSRN-Abstract 119684, Social Science Research Network, April 16, 2008. Accessed 20 June 2015.

Agabi, Justice Godwin Kanu. 2002. Prohibition of Discriminatory Punishments. A Letter Written to All the Twelve States That Apply Sharia Law, on March 18, 2002.

Ahmad, Siddiqi. n.d. *Sahih Muslim*, trans. Beirut: Dar al-Arabia; Ali, Yusuf. 1983. *The Qur'an: Translation and Commentary*. Maryland: Amana Corp.

Ahmad ibn Muhammad, Al-Qastalani Shihab al-Din. n.d. *Irshad al-Sari: Sharh Sahih al-Bukrari,* vol. 8. Beirut: Dar Sadir.

Ajetummobi, Musa Ali. 1988. Shari`ah Legal Practice in Nigeria: 1956–83. Ph.D dissertation, University of Ilorin, Department of Islamic Studies, June.

Akinade, Akintunde. 2014. *Christian Responses to Islam in Nigeria: A Contextual Study of Ambivalent Encounters*. New York: Palgrave Macmillan.

Al-Dirdir, Abu al-Barakat Ahmad ibn Muhammad ibn Ahmad. 1972. *Al-Sharh al-Saghir 'ala Aqrab al-Masalik ila Madhhab al-Imam Maliki*. Cairo: Dar al_Ma'arif.

Al-Faruqi, Lamya. 1988. *Women, Muslims, and Islam*. Indianapolis: American Trust Publication.

Al-Faruqi, Isma'il. 1986. *The Cultural Atlas of Islam*. New York: Macmillan Publishing Co.

Al-Ghazali, Muhammad. 1976. *Fiqh al-Sirah*. Cairo: Dar al-Kutub al-Hadithah.

Y. Sodiq, *A History of the Application of Islamic Law in Nigeria*,
DOI 10.1007/978-3-319-50600-5

Al-Hafid, Abu al-Walid Ahmad Muhammad ibn Rushd. 1960. *Bidayat al-Mujtahid wa Nihayat al-Muqtasid*. Cairo: Matba'at Mustafa al-Babi.

Al-Nawawi, Yahya ibn Sharaf al-Din. 1960. *Sahih Muslim bi Sharh al-Nawawi*. Cairo: Al-Matba'at al- Misriyah.

Al-Shafi'i, Muhammad ibn Idris. 1973. *Al-Umm*. Beirut: Dar al-Ma'rifah.

Al-Shafi'i, Muhammad bin Idris. 1987. *Al-Risala fi Usul al-Fiqh*. [Treatise on the Foundations of Islamic Jurisprudence], translated with an introduction, notes and appendices by Majid Khadduri, 2nd ed. Cambridge: Islamic Texts Society.

Al-Shatibi, Abu Ishaq Ibrahim bin Musa. 1922. *Al-Muwafaqaat fi Usul al-Ahkam*. Cairo: Matba Matba' at al-Salafiyyah.

Al-Shawkani, Muhammad bin Ali bin Muhammad. 1961. *Nayl al-Awtar Sharh Muntaqa alAkhbar min Ahadith Sayyid al-Anam*. Cairo: Matba'at Mustafa al-Babi al-Halabi.

Al-Zuhayli, Wahbah. 1986. *Al-Figh al-Islami wa Adilatuhu*. Beirut: Dar al-Fikr.

Anderson, J.N.D. 1954. *Islamic Law in Africa*, 175. London: Colonial Research Publication.

Arafah, Al-Dasuki Shaykh Muhammad. 1980. *Hashiyat al-Dasuki 'Ala Al-Sharh al-Kabir*. Isa al-Babi al-Halabi wa Sharkah: Cairo.

Ayoub, Mahmoud. 1989. Roots of Muslim-Christian Conflicts. *The Muslim World* 79: 25–45.

Baderin, Mashood. The Shari`ah Alteration: The Moral and Legal Questions. www.nigeriaworld.com. Accessed 5 May 2012.

Balogun, Ismail. 1975. *The Life and Works of Uthman Dan Fodio*. Lagos: Islamic Publishing Bureau.

Barnes, Andrew. 2004. Religious Insult: Christian Critiques of Islam and the Government in Colonial Northern Nigeria. *Journal of Religion in Africa* 34(1&2): 62–81.

Barrett, David. 1997. Annual Statistical Table on Global Mission. *International Bulletin* 20(1): 24–25.

Basri, Ghazali. 1994. *Nigeria and shari`ah*. Leicester: The Islamic Foundation.

Bello, Mohammed. 2002. Obstacles Before *Sharia*. www.nigeriaworld, posted on February 12, 2002. Accessed 3 May 2012.

Boer, Jan. 2000. The Nigerian Christian – Muslim Stand – Off: Some Underlying Issues, Parameters for a Solution. *TCNN Research Bulletin*, 33/2000 (40th Anniversary Issue): 4–23.

Brenner, Louis. 1979. Muhammad Amin al-Kanam_and Religion and Politics in Bornu. In *Studies in West African Islamic History*, ed. John Ralph Willis. Totowa: Frank Cass.

Burdon, J.A. 1972. *Northern Nigeria: Historical Notes on Certain Emirates and Tribes*. London: Farnborough, Gregg. (reprint).

Burns, Alan C. 1948. *History of Nigeria*. London: George Allen & Unwin Ltd.

Christelow, Allen. 1987. Three Islamic Voices in Contemporary Nigeria. In *Islam and Political Economy of Meaning: Comparative Studies of Muslim Discourse*, ed. William R. Roff. London: Croom Helm.

Clarke, Peter B. 1982. *West Africa and Islam*. London: Edward Arnold Ltd.

Constitution of the Federal Republic of Nigeria, 1999.

Crocker, W.R. 1936. *A Critique of British Colonial Administration*. London: George Allen & Unwin Ltd.

Crowder, Michael Ajayi. 1966. *A Short History of Nigeria*. New York: Frederich A. Praeger.

Denny, Frederick M. 1987. *Islam and the Muslim Community*. San Franscisco: Harper & Row Publishers.

Duff, Mark. Nigerian Man Faces Death for Penalty. *BBC News*, June 27, 2002. http://news.bbc.co.uk/1/hi/world/africa/2070594.html.

Esposito, John. 1998. *Islam: The Straight Path*. 2nd ed. New York: Oxford University Press.

Esposito, John, and Y. Haddad. 1998. *Islam and Gender in Islam*. Oxford: Oxford University Press.

Esposito, John L. 2002. *Unholy War: Terror in the Name of Islam*. Oxford: Oxford University Press.

Faruki, Kemal A. 1975. *Islamic Jurisprudence*. Lahore: National Book Foundation.

Gbadamosi, T.G.O. 1978. *The Growth of Islam Among the Yoruba, 1841–1908*, Ibadan History Series. London/Atlantic Highlands: Longman/Humanities Press.

Ghazali, Abu Hamid Muhammad bin Muhammad. 1937. *Al-Mustasfa min 'Ilm al-Usul*. Cairo: Matba 'at al-Amiriyyah.

Glasse, Cyril. 1989. *The Concise Encyclopedia of Islam*. San Franscisco: Harper & Row, Publishers Inc.

Goddard, Hugh. 1995. *Christians & Muslims: From Double Standard to Mutual Understanding*. Surrey: Curzon Press.

Greene, A.H.M. 1968. *Lugard and the Amalgamation of Nigeria: A Documentary Record*. London: Frank Cass & Co. Ltd.

Gwandu, A.A. 1986. Aspects of the Administration of Justice in the Sokoto Caliphate and Shaykh Abdullah Ibn Fodio's Contribution to it. In *Islamic Law in Nigeria: Application & Teaching*, ed. S.K. Rashid. Lagos: Islamic Publication Bureau.

Gwarzo, Hasan. *The Development of the Implementation of Shari`ah in the Northern States*. Paper Presented at a Seminar Organized by the Department of Islamic Studies in Cooperation with the Department of Arabic and Faculty of Law, Bayero University, Kano, on 23 March 1985, p. 6.

Haddad, Y.Y. and Haddad, Wadi Z, eds. 1995. *Christian-Muslim Encounters*. Gainesville: University Press of Florida.

Hallaq, Wael. 1997. *A History of Islamic Legal Theories*. Cambridge: Cambridge University Press.

Hamilton, Charles. 1982. *The Hedaya or Guide: A Commentary on the Mussulman Laws*. Delhi: Islamic Book Trust.

Haruna, Mohammad. 2000. *Sharia*: Where the Solution Lies. *Today Newspaper*, April 16–22.

Hasan, Ahmad. 1978. *The Doctrine of Ijma' in Islam*. Islamabad: Islamic Research Institute.

Hauwa, Ibrahim. 2004. Rules of Law Prevails in the Case of Amina Lawal. *Human Rights Brief* 11(3): 39–41.

Haykal, Muhammad Husayn. 1976. *The Life of Muhammad* (trans: al Faruqi, Ismail Ragi). Plainfield: American Trust Publication.

Hiskett, Mervyn. 1984. *The Development of Islam in West Africa*. London: Longman.

Hogben, S.J. 1967. *An Introduction to the History of Islamic States of Northern Nigeria*. Ibadan: Oxford University Press.

Ibn Anas, Imam Malik. 1963. *Al-Mudawwanah al-Kubra*. Cairo: al-Matba'at al-Khayriyyah.

———. 1967. *Muwatta'Malik*. Beirut: Mu'asasat Dar al-Tahrir li Tiba'ah wa al-Nashr.

Ibn Hajar al-Haythanmi, Ahmad bin Muhammad. n.d. *Tuhfat al-Muhtaj fi sharh al-Minhaj*. Beirut: Dar Ihya al-turath al-Arabi.

Ibn Idris al-Shafi'i, Al-Imam Muhammad. 1987. *Al-Risala fi Usul al-Fiqh*. [Treatise on The Foundations of Islamic Jurispredence], translated with an introduction/Notes and appendices by Majid Khadduri, 2nd. Cambridge: Islamic Texts Society.

Ibn Rush al-Hafid, Abu al-Walid Ahmad Muhammad ibn Rushd. 1960. *Bidayat al-Mujtahid wa Nihayat al-Muqtasid*. Cairo: Matba'at Mustafa al-Babi.

Isa Shani, Alhaji Ma'ji, Hussain Ahangar, and Mohammad Altaf. 1986. Marriage Guardianship in Islam: Reflection on a Recent Nigeria Judgement. *Islamic And Comparative Law Quarterly* 6(4): 278.

Kamali, H. Mohammad. 1991. *Principles of Islamic Jurisprudence*. Cambridge: Islamic Texts Society.

Keffi, Sheikh U. D. *Improving the Quality of Life of Muslims Through the Implementation of Socio-Economic Aspects of Sharia in Nigeria*. Paper Presented at the Conference on Women's Rights and Access to Justice Under the Sharia in Northern Nigeria, Held at Abuja on February 26–27, 2003.

Kenny, Joseph. 1986. Shari'a in Nigeria: A Historical Survey. *Bulletin on Islam and Christian-Muslim Relations in Africa* 4: 1–21.

———. 1996. Sharia and Christianity in Nigeria: Islam and a Secular State. *Journal of Religion in Africa* 26(4): 338–364.

Kumar, Sanjib. http://publishyourarticles.net/knowledge-hub/law/what-is-the-Difference-between-law-and-morality/4207. Accessed 11 May 2016.

Last, Murray. 1967. *The Sokoto Caliphate.* New York: Humanities Press.

———. 2007. Muslims and Christians in Nigeria: An Economy of Political Panic. *The Round Table* 96(392): 605–616.

Lawal, Nike S., Matthew N.O. Sadiku, and Ade Dopanu. 2004. *Understanding Yoruba Life and Culture.* Trenton: Africa World Press Inc.

Lawan Yusufari, Mamman A. 1997. The Application of Islamic Law in Nigeria. *Yearbook of Islamic and Middle Eastern Law on Line* 4(1): 201–209.

Lewis, Bernard. 1993. *Islam and the West.* New York: Oxford University Press.

Ludwig, Frieder. 2008. Christian Muslim Relations in Northern Nigeria Since the Introduction of *Shari`ah* in 1999. *Journal of the American Academy of Religion* 76(3): 602–637.

Luggard, Lord Fredrick. 1970. *Political Memoranda.* London: Frank & Cass Co. Ltd.

Mahmassani, R. Sobhi. 1961. *Falsafat al-Tashri fi al-Islam* (The Philosophy of Jurisprudence in Islam) (trans: Ziadeh, Farhat J.). Leiden: E. J. Brill.

Mahmud, Abdul Malik Bappa. 1988. *A Brief History of Shari`ah in the Defunct Northern Nigeria.* Jos: Jos University Press.

Mala, Sam Babs. *The Shari`ah and the Treatment of Non-Muslims: A Justified Fear Among Nigerians.* Unpublished Manuscript, p. 1.

Mbahi, Muhammad. *Sharia,* Northern Ethnic and Religious Minority and the Federal Government: A Perspective, posted at: www.nigeriaworld.com, August 10, 2001. Accessed 3 May 2002.

Mohammad, Ovey N. 1999. *Muslim – Christian Relations: Past, Present, Future.* New York: Orbis Books.

Motin, Rashid A. 1987. Political Dynamism of Islam in Nigeria. *Islamic Studies* 26(2): 180.

Nasr, H. 1972. *Islam, Ideals, and Realities.* Boston: Beacon Press.

Nyang, Sulayman S. 1984. *Islam, Christianity and African Identity.* Vermont: Amana Books.

———. 1999. *Islam in the United States of America.* Chicago: ABC International Group, Inc.

Obilade, A.O. 1979. *The Nigerian Legal System.* London: Sweet & Maxwell.

Oloyede, Ishaq O. 1987. *Mukhtasar Khalil* and the Understanding of Islamic Law in Nigeria. *Hamdard Islamicus* 12(1): 83–90.

Owhonda, John. 1998. *Nigeria: A Nation of Many Peoples.* Parsippany: Dillon Press.

Peters, Peters. 1979. *Islam and Colonialism: The Doctrine of Jihad in Modern History.* New York: Mouton Publishers.

Qadri, Ansar A. 1981. *Islamic Jurisprudence in the Modern World. Pakistan.* Lahore: Sh. Muhammad Ashraf.

Rahman, Fazlur. 1965. *Islamic Methodology in History*. Karachi: Central Institute of Islamic Research.
Rashd, S.K. ed. 1986. *Islamic Law in Nigeria*. Lagos: Islamic Publication Bureau.
Report of the Constitution Drafting Committee Containing the Draft Constitution for the Federal Republic of Nigeria (Lagos, 1976) Sec. 180–186.
Ruxton, F.H. 1980. *Maliki Law*. Connecticut: Hyperion Press, Inc.
Sabiq, Sayyid. 1969. *Fiqh as-Sunnah*. Beirut: Dar al-Kitab al-Arabi.
———. 1985. *Fiqh as-Sunnah*, 22. Beirut: Dar al-Kitab al-Arabi.
Sambo, Muhammad Bashir. 1986. *Shari`ah in a Multi-Religious State: Its Application and Mimitations*. Paper Presented at the Association of Nigerian Legal Practitioners Held in Lagos, February.
Schacht, Joseph. 1967. *The Origins of Muhammadan Jurisprudence*. Oxford: The Clarendon Press.
Schwarz, Frederick A.O. 1965. *Nigeria: The Tribes, the Nation, or the Race – The Politics of Independence*. Cambridge, MA: The M.I.T Press.
Shittu, Mujahid Hamza. 2014. A Review of the Activities of Christian Missionary, Clergy, Experts and Writers on Islam in Nigeria. *Journal of Islamic Studies and Culture* 2(3): 25–46.
Smith, M.G. 1964. The Jihad of Shehu Dan Fodio: Some Problem. In *Islam in Tropical Africa*, ed. I.M. Lewis. Bloomington: Indiana University Press.
Sodiq, Yushau. 1992. A History of Islamic Law in Nigeria: Past and Present. *Islamic Studies* 31: 85–108.
———. 1996. An Analysis of Yoruba and Islamic Laws of Inheritance. *Muslim World* 86: 313–333.
———. 2004. Ijtihad: The Art of Cracking the Nuts. In *The Nigerian Journal of Islamic Political Thought*, Department of Islamic Law, Faculty of Law, University of Ilorin, Ilorin, Nigeria 1(1): 1–61.
———. 2007. African Muslims in the United States: The Nigerian Case. In *African Immigrant Religions in America*, ed. Jacob Olupona and Gemihnani Regina. New York: New York University Press.
———. 2009. Can Muslims and Christians Live Together Peacefully in Nigeria? *Muslim World* 99(4): 646–688.
———. 2010. *An Insider's Guide to Islam*. Indianapolis: Trafford Publishing.
Statement by the Government of the Norther Region of Nigeria on the RE-Organization of the Legal and Judicial Systems of the Northern Region. (SGNRNRLJSNR) Kaduna, Government Printer, 1958, par. 36
Sulaiman, Ibraheem. 1986. *A Revolution in History: The Jihad of Uthman Dan Fodio*. New York: Mansell Publishing Ltd.
———. 1987. *The Islamic State and the Challenge of History*. New York: Mansell Publishing Ltd.
The Constitution of the Federation of Nigeria as amended by the Constitution Assembly 2, decree 1976. See Olilade, pp. 176–77.

The *Shari`ah* Court of Appeal Law (N.N. Laws 1963).

Usman, Yusuf Bala. 1979. The Transformation of Political Communities: Some Notes On the Perception of a Significant Dimension of the Sokoto Jihad. In *Studies in the History of The Sokoto Caliphate.* (Ahmadu Bello University, Zaria, Department of Religion, 1979), pp. 34–55.

Uthman Dan Fodio, Shaykh. n.d. *Ihya al-Sunnah wa Ikhmad al-Bid'a, Tawqif al-Muslimin 'ala Hukm Madhhab al-Mujtahidin, and Irshad al-Ummah.*

Williams, Rotimi. 1977. Proceedings of the Constituent Assembly Official Report, Federal Ministry of Information, Lagos, no. Z, November 1, 1977, p. 9.

Ya Alkali, Justice Kui. 1989. *The Area Courts in Kano State.* Paper Presented at the 1989 Law Week at Faculty of Law, Bayero University, Kano, May 31 1989, pp. 1–3.

Yadudu, Auwalu H. 2006. *Evaluating the Implementation of Shariah in Nigeria: Challenges and Limiting Factors Revisited.* Paper presented at the National Conference on Leadership, State & Society Under the Shari`ah In Nigeria: The Dividends. Held in Abuja, Nigeria on July 10–12, 2006.

Yawuri, Aliyu Musa. On Defending Safiyatu Husaini and Amina Lawal. In *Shari`ah Implementation in Northern Nigeria: A Source Book*, 1996–2006, ed. Philip Ostein, et al. (Ibadan, Nigeria: Spectrum Books Limited, 2007), vol. 5: 133, 139.

Yusuf, Ahmad Beita. 1976. Legal Pluralism in the Northern States of Nigeria: Conflict of Laws in a Multi-Ethic Environment. Unpublished Ph.D dissertation, State University of New York, Buffalo, p. 46.

Yusuf, Salahu-deen. 1987. The Press and Islam in Nigeria: A Critical Appraisal of the Impact of Western Press on Some Nigerian Newspaper Media on Issues Relating to Islam and the Muslims. M.A. thesis, Dept. of Islamic Studies, Bayero University, Kano, p. 67.

———. Education in Nigeria. See World Education News and Reviews, Published on July 1, 2013. Access at: www.wenr.wes.org on 12 June 2015.

Index[1]

[1] Note: Page numbers followed by "n" refers to notes.

Y. Sodiq, *A History of the Application of Islamic Law in Nigeria*,
DOI 10.1007/978-3-319-50600-5

FSC
www.fsc.org
MIX
Papier | Fördert
gute Waldnutzung
FSC® C083411

Kolibri 360 GmbH
Ferdinand-Jühlke-Straße 7
99095 Erfurt, Deutschland
produktsicherheit@kolibri360.de